RESISTERS

52 YOUNG WOMEN
MAKING HERSTORY
RIGHT NOW

First published in Great Britain in 2019 by Wren & Rook
Text copyright © Lauren Sharkey, 2019
Illustration copyright © Manjit Thapp, 2019
Design copyright © Hodder & Stoughton Limited, 2019
All rights reserved.

The right of Lauren Sharkey and Manjit Thapp to be identified as the author and illustrator respectively of this Work has been asserted by them in accordance with the Copyright, Designs & Patents Act 1988.

ISBN: 9781526361844
E-book ISBN: 9781526361851

10 9 8 7 6 5 4 3 2 1

Wren & Rook
An imprint of
Hachette Children's Group
Part of Hodder & Stoughton
Carmelite House
50 Victoria Embankment
London EC4Y 0DZ

An Hachette UK Company
www.hachette.co.uk
www.hachettechildrens.co.uk

Publishing Director: Debbie Foy
Senior Editor: Laura Horsley
Art Director: Laura Hambleton
Designed by Thy Bui

Printed and bound by the CPI Group (UK) Ltd, Croydon, CR0 4YY

Source on page 197: Lorde, Audre, "When in doubt ...", *A Burst of Light*, Firebrand Books, 1988.

Picture acknowledgements: The publisher would like to thank the following for permission to reproduce their pictures and photographs: Alyssa Carson (original photograph © Designual), Amika George (original photograph © Sophia Spring), Asha and Ima Christian, Diana Sirokai, Ella Fields, Gitanjali Rao, Sage Grace Dolan-Sandrino, Jasilyn Charger (original photograph © Zeb Pits), Maddy Rasmussen (original photograph © Kaily Fitzgerald), Maya Ghazal (original photograph © Neequaye Dreph Dsane), MC Soffia (original photograph © Brechó Replay), Melati and Isabel Wijsen, Nawaal Akram (original photograph © Maria's Photoclicks) and Taylor Richardson (original photograph © Latonja Richardson).

LAUREN SHARKEY

MANJIT THAPP

RESISTERS

52 YOUNG WOMEN
MAKING HERSTORY
RIGHT NOW

CONTENTS

INTRODUCTION

Now more than ever, girls across the world are uniting to stand up for what they believe in, to make their voices heard, and to create change that will last forever. Whether they are protesting against period poverty, defending transgender rights, championing body positivity, or campaigning for gun control, they are all battling relentlessly to improve the lives of people everywhere. This book is written for everyone who wants to join them – the girls, women, boys and men who all play a role in changing the world as we know it.

This may seem like a tall order, especially when the news is awash with so much negativity, but the 52 young women documented in this book are proof that you can fight for your rights in the face of criticism and that no online troll can knock you down.

Some of the featured campaigners are active in the worlds of politics, education, and the arts. Others work to promote science, conservation, and LGBTQ+ rights. And they all represent different corners of the globe – from the US to Indonesia, the UK to Australia, and Syria to Brazil. But whether they're taking on the rigid views of what women should look like and how they should behave, or the stereotypes that surround issues of religion, race and mental health, their efforts are all making a difference.

Just take Wadi Ben-Hirki and Memory Banda. Fed up of the way girls' rights were being stripped away in parts of Africa, they each created their own organisations to eliminate child marriage and fight for female education. And best of all, people are listening and change is happening! It's a similar story for 16-year-old Isabel Wijsen and her older sister Melati. Together, they helped convince the government of Bali to ban plastic bags and save the ocean. Next stop, they'll be helping save the world.

Each and every one of these young activist's campaigns are unique, proving just how many issues women still have to contend with in the modern age. That's because despite our best efforts, gender inequality is still a prominent problem across the globe. Women are still paid less than men and, on top of that, still have to fork out for the pink tax. This is when products marketed at women are sold for a higher price than the exact same product designed for a man. It often applies to everyday items such as deodorants and razors, as well as clothing and even underwear. Have a look when you're next in the supermarket and compare the prices between male and female products – you'll soon start seeing the pink tax! And then there's the cost of having a period too. If you're female, have you ever worked out how much you will spend on tampons, sanitary pads, menstrual cups, and those all-important spare knickers over your lifetime? I have, and it's enough for quite a few sunny holidays.

Some women, however, do have more freedom than others. In several countries around the world, girls and women don't have a choice when it comes to their own bodies or their own destinies. Activists who are native to these countries are working to change that and have been joined by more Resisters from other parts of the world.

These young campaigners aren't just working to make the world a better place for women either. They are improving the lives of people of all races, religions and sexualities. That's because the more we use our voices and skills to fight for what we believe in, the more equality can thrive, so that one day law enforcement won't get away with violence when they encounter certain communities on the streets. People won't pick on someone because they are wearing a hijab. And people won't be discriminated against because they choose to love someone of the same sex or because they don't identify as the person laid out on their birth certificate.

Working together is key to improving society and it's the one thing that all of the following stories have in common. Each of the young women in this book may have worked alone at some point in their journey, but only by partnering up with a friend, family member, or thousands of people online could they kickstart their revolution. This community gave them the strength they needed when things got rough. It supported them when they struggled to balance school with the work they deemed to be more important. And it energised them to keep going.

Nobody said being an activist was easy. You might experience negativity online or from certain people in real life, whether your campaign is hugely controversial or not. There will be days when you feel hopeless and can't bear to look at social media. There will be days when you feel like

your efforts just aren't enough and that change is impossible. But, know that nothing is impossible. Absorb the advice of the activists in this book and try to remember it every single day. Learn from their struggles and use their triumphs to guide you when you're feeling lost. And find your own community of campaigners too. Ask them questions and let them support you when you become overwhelmed.

It's been a pleasure compiling this book and weaving together the voices of so many brilliant young activists, but it's been a personal learning exercise too. I am a young white woman, meaning I have dealt with my fair share of sexism and my age has often convinced people they have the right to dismiss me. But it also means I was born with a certain kind of privilege. I haven't experienced discrimination because of my skin colour, because of a disability, or because of my parents' income. That is why I've worked to amplify the voices of so many women from so many backgrounds. I asked them to speak their truth and gave them a space to shape their story. But more importantly, I learned that being a true ally means learning to listen. To discard all of my preconceived ideas about how I thought I could best help people and let them tell me how to help instead.

For too long, women have been silenced and forcibly held back, but a change is happening and it's happening now. We need to speak up against the injustices we face every single day. We need to create change. We need to resist. And together, we might just make the planet a better place.

So, are you ready to join the Resisters?

FEMINISM and EQUALITY

What does feminism mean? Well, to me, feminism is the belief that everyone is equal and deserves to be treated in that way. And who wouldn't want that? But unfortunately, our society has been built on old-fashioned patriarchal values, which means a lot of the things that exist today favour boys and men. Here's a few examples: girls living in certain parts of the world are still expected to give up their ambitions to become wives and mothers. Men still dominate some of the planet's most powerful industries while women are barely given a chance to succeed. And, thanks to laws created by men, some women still don't have control over their own reproductive health. These issues are historical and, although some are definitely changing for the better, there is still a long way to go until both genders are treated the same.

In fact, inequality exists across the world: at the time of writing, 130 million girls are unable to go to school, 12 million girls are forced into child marriage each year, and one in three women will experience sexual violence in their lifetime. Choice is an important word that is often overlooked when it comes to women. In some countries, many girls can't go to school even if they want to, with issues such as poverty or local traditions that mean they are expected to look after their home, often standing in their way.

But imagine life without education. If you can't read and communicate your ideas, your choices and future become quite limited. Many girls in these circumstances face few employment opportunities, getting married at a very young age or having children before they are ready. In other places, a different type of failure is happening. A lack of sexual and reproductive education services mean topics such as consent and sexual abuse aren't being taught far and wide. Some girls are unable to access sanitary products, meaning they miss out on doing normal things when they menstruate each month. And in places like the US, many are finding it increasingly hard to access abortion clinics, travelling for hours on end to seek a legal and safe place.

But things can and will change so that women are given equal opportunities that allow them to thrive in every aspect of their lives – no matter where they are from or what they look like. The following activists are passionate about just that and are working tirelessly to get there. Let's look at the way they are resisting ...

AMIKA GEORGE, 19

PERIOD POVERTY CAMPAIGNER, CREATOR OF #FREEPERIODS

Once a woman starts getting her period, she will inevitably need sanitary products – whether it be tampons, pads, a Mooncup or anything else out there that will do the job of soaking up the blood. But would you believe that one study has shown that women will spend over £18,000 on their periods in their lifetime! Nineteen-year-old Amika George agrees that this is a ridiculous amount and is doing something about it.

After reading how some girls in the UK were missing school due to the unaffordable cost of sanitary products, Amika decided to do more research in to the concept of period poverty. She found that the high cost of period products mean that girls from low-income families simply cannot afford to buy them and are forced to use toilet roll or scraps of fabric in their knickers each month. Sometimes, they miss school altogether out of sheer embarrassment. Of course this isn't just a Western issue either, but a problem across the entire globe ...

But the reason it is such a significant problem in the UK is because of the so-called tampon tax in which the government actually classes sanitary products as luxury items. Essentially, this means you have to pay more for them. Of course, the idea of tampons being a "luxury" item has angered a lot of women because there is no luxury in having a period and sanitary products are a necessity! But it also means more and more girls and their families are struggling financially.

In 2017, Amika launched a petition urging the UK government to provide free period products in schools for struggling girls. She then held a march in London where more than two thousand people turned up with politicians and celebrities taking to the stage to speak about the importance of #FreePeriods.

Since then, there has been progress. Some stores have agreed to reduce the price of sanitary items while Scotland decided to provide free sanitary products to all students. The UK government also gave £1.5 million to help combat period poverty, and Amika was one of the youngest campaigners who convinced them.

Despite these achievements, Amika isn't stopping until girls everywhere can go about their everyday lives without worrying about their periods and ensuring they can afford the products they need during that time of their cycle.

AMIKA

Periods are still a conversation killer. I grew up in a family where I could speak about periods openly, but I know that's not the case in many households. I've seen faces glow red when I tell them about #FreePeriods and the subject is often changed in a flash.

People need to know that period poverty is happening across the globe. It's damaging the lives of girls as young as ten and is forcing some, who are living in countries such as India and Kenya, to drop out of school altogether. Girls in the UK meanwhile are missing school for up to a week every month just because they can't afford to buy pads or tampons. Others are fashioning their own makeshift pads using socks stuffed with wads of toilet paper or old clothes.

When families face the choice between eating and heating, period protection becomes an unattainable luxury. Many girls told me that they didn't want to ask their parents for money to buy pads; they knew there wasn't any to give. I could see it was preventing girls from achieving their ambitions and robbing them of their childhoods. It was wrong on every level, and so I decided that I would try and raise awareness of period poverty as much as I could.

I started the #FreePeriods campaign, set up a petition, contacted politicians and journalists, and decided to team up with my amazing friends, Scarlett Curtis and Grace Campbell of The Pink Protest. We decided to organise a protest; it was a way of reaching out to the government to say they couldn't keep ignoring period poverty and that they had to give provision to girls from low-income families — I wanted them to hear the rallying cries for change.

Part of my campaign is to destigmatise menstruation. We should be celebrating our periods and embracing the fact that our bodies are so incredible. Today, in rural Nepal, women are still banished to outdoor huts when they are having their period as they're seen as unclean. There's even a belief that if a menstruating woman touches a fruit tree, it might never bear fruit!

Social media has been key for our campaign. It's a really powerful tool, which allows us to mobilise and galvanise, to spread a message at the click of a button, and make people feel as if it's their campaign too. I started #FreePeriods from my bedroom and I'm astounded every day at how widespread it has become.

It's been difficult to stay on top of my A-levels. Organising the protest while sorting out my university applications was something of a challenge. But I wouldn't have it any other way. Whenever I start to flag, I get the strength I need from someone who tells me they're going through period poverty and how much they need things to change.

My advice is to find like-minded people
who you can draw from in terms of IDEAS
and INSPIRATION. And BE BOLD.
Go three steps beyond what feels acceptable
and KEEP PUSHING. Try and get exposure for
your cause in a MAINSTREAM publication
and be as VOCAL as you can possibly be.

In the future, I'd like to see young people being included in decision-making processes. Our voices count and are valuable. I hope that we live in a fairer society where women are treated equally. I hope that young girls have the self-belief to feel that they can do anything.

As for periods? It may take years to implement policies that eradicate period poverty altogether, if at all, but the government needs to find solutions to help pockets of society in small ways and make sure girls have no reason to miss out on education because of their menstruation cycle. Right now, it's tragic, unjust, and downright unacceptable.

MEMORY BANDA, 22

ANTI-CHILD-MARRIAGE CAMPAIGNER

When Memory Banda's sister Mercy was 11, she fell pregnant and was forced to marry the father of her child. By the time Mercy was 16, she had been married twice, had three children, and had to put her dream of becoming a teacher on hold.

Almost half of the girls living in Malawi are given no choice but to marry, often to men two or three times their age, and are destined to live a life of motherhood and little else. But not anymore, thanks to Memory.

As a young teen, Memory discovered Malawi's Girls Empowerment Network; an organisation that has been fighting to ban child marriage. She volunteered with them, learning how to convince girls in her village to open up and present their stories to village leaders. She then bombarded government officials with their stories of forced and early marriages until the legal marriage age was raised from 15 to 18. When communities found a loophole in this law that allowed child marriage to continue with parental consent, Memory and her fellow campaigners brought a petition with thousands of signatures to the government, persuading them to amend the constitution and stop people from ignoring the issue once and for all.

The fight for female equality is far from over but, to Memory and the other members of her very own foundation, at least it has begun!

MEMORY

In Malawi, social norms and cultural values still stop girls from reaching their full potential. As a girl growing up in such an environment, I have witnessed different forms of social injustice. I have seen my family members and classmates drop out of school and girls as young as 11 being married off.

Once girls reach puberty, they are supposed to undergo the tradition of Chinamwali. Here they go to a camp, away from the village, for a week and are taught about growing up and how they can be a productive member of society. However, the girls are also often introduced to a culture that treats them like sexual objects. Chinamwali teaches a twisted and age-inappropriate form of sexual education, which can result in these young girls being sexually abused. Any actual sex education they do receive is also quite limited. For example, they don't have information on contraceptives, leading to an increase in early pregnancy. A huge percentage of girls are also forced to marry young, increasing the school dropout rate.

Witnessing a child getting married is the most hurtful thing to watch. When my little sister was forced to marry after falling pregnant, her dreams were shattered. I therefore decided to stand up and speak out about the challenges that girls face.

Girls should be given an education and not a husband; girls must be given equal opportunities. I feel privileged to have been able to challenge the status quo and want to continue to change girls' stories from being victims to survivors.

But I couldn't have done it without the Girls Empowerment Network. They gave me an opportunity to connect with more young girls and a safe space to discuss issues that affected us. There were times when people resisted us and we met setbacks, but the project was a success. We managed to persuade village leaders to pass the first community bylaws which secured girls' rights to an education and ensured they would no longer have to face abusive traditions.

The government's law change, however, has been the biggest step towards ending child marriage. It prohibits any marriages below the age of 18 and also means girls are more empowered and able to defend their rights. More girls are now completing primary and secondary school too. In fact, today my sister is back at school. The new laws have changed her life and status.

Recently, I started my own organisation, Foundation4Girls Leadership. It's dedicated to raising girl leaders and allows them to network with activists, identifying critical injustices and acting collectively to solve them. We're implementing a back-to-school programme for girls and young women who left school due to early marriage and teen pregnancy, and are providing psychosocial support to victims and survivors of child marriage. My ultimate goal is to build a Girls' Leadership Academy where girls will be given the skills to become agents of change and contribute to the development of our country.

I have become unstoppable and now realise that being young doesn't mean you cannot influence change.

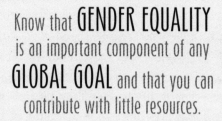
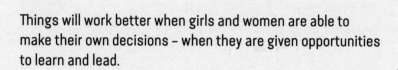

Know that **GENDER EQUALITY** is an important component of any **GLOBAL GOAL** and that you can contribute with little resources.

Things will work better when girls and women are able to make their own decisions – when they are given opportunities to learn and lead.

WADI BEN-HIRKI, 22

CHILD EDUCATION CAMPAIGNER, FOUNDER OF THE WADI BEN-HIRKI FOUNDATION

When one of Wadi Ben-Hirki's close friends got married when she was still in primary school, Wadi knew she couldn't remain silent any longer. One day her friend was enjoying an education, the next she wasn't. But it wasn't just Wadi's best friend: many girls around her were being treated poorly and violently too.

So, when she was just 18, she set up a non-profit organisation. The Wadi Ben-Hirki Foundation fights to provide an education for all the children living in northern Nigeria; a place that has some of the worst illiteracy and poverty rates in the world. Her foundation runs numerous campaigns throughout the area, which include moving children from the streets into school, stopping female genital mutilation, campaigning against children being forced into marriage, and helping young people in areas that have been hit by war. So far, over three thousand children have benefitted.

Wadi now speaks on global stages and has been recognised by humanitarian awards, including Philanthropist of the Year at the Nigerian Teen Choice Awards. Her belief is that the longer people are left in the dark, the longer it will take for those who are suffering to see the light. She therefore continues to campaign and expose how women and girls are denied the right to a decent life – but hopes that thousands more will see their lives transformed in the coming years.

WADI

Nigeria and Africa are facing a lot of challenges. The poverty and population rates are increasing and there are little to no resources for everyone. The government hasn't prioritised education either and so even in the places where education is free, it's not of a good quality. This means I have witnessed many people graduate from school that are still unable to speak English or even write their names.

But it's important for girls to have an education so that they can escape the cycle of poverty. If a woman isn't educated, her children will likely not be educated either as she can't pass down her knowledge. This ripple effect means many grow up to be illiterate and end up going to extremes to survive – sometimes even through prostitution or armed robbery.

I was a very smart child. I learned faster than most of my mates and I loved to read books, dictionaries and maps. I didn't have the normal luxury that many children had but I was privileged to have parents who believed I deserved a right to a good life and to quality education.

I remember discovering that a close friend of mine in primary school had been married off all of a sudden. She was eight or nine years old. Can you imagine? At that young age, what could a girl possibly know? I then found out many girls were being treated badly in my local area and some men were beating up their wives. A woman is a human being first, before anything else, so why would she be treated any differently?

At the age of ten, I came across a documentary about Oprah Winfrey. She shared her life story and how she was able to rise above and beyond the poverty and abuse that she experienced at a young age. I drew strength from her — especially because I realised we shared the same birthday!

In 2015, I started the organisation. I was tired of what was going on and wanted to be the change that I was seeking.

I started **LITTLE BY LITTLE** because little drops make an **OCEAN**.

Now, my foundation runs four major projects. The first project, #Street2School, advocates for education, offers scholarships to outstanding children, and teaches them skills to make money and cater for their families. Forty-three per cent of girls in Nigeria marry before they're 18 so the second project, #GirlsNotWives, advocates against child marriage, female genital mutilation, gender-based violence, and trafficking.

The third is #LITMOW which stands for Love In The Midst Of War. I come from the war-stricken part of Nigeria where many people have lost their lives and property. This project seeks to rehabilitate survivors of violent uprisings and show them love. It aims to teach people how they can help themselves with the little resources they have, and to unite people to see the beauty and diversity in one another.

The last project, #Sheroes, aims to empower women and turn their struggles into strengths. It's an avenue to help victimised and marginalised girls aspire for greatness and not be limited by their circumstances or who the world defines them as.

Some people say I'm too young to do this, too ambitious, too dreamy. But the bigger picture is all I see.

My age is inspiring other girls to
DREAM BIG and believe
they can do whatever they
PUT THEIR MINDS TO.

Knowing that this work is far greater than me and about the thousands and possibly millions of people whose lives will be affected is what keeps me going.

If you want to make a difference, you must put in the work. I'd love to see a world that lets go of every single thing that tries to tear us apart. If we join hands and work together, these things are all achievable.

Stories will be told about the heroines of our generation. You should make sure you're one of them!

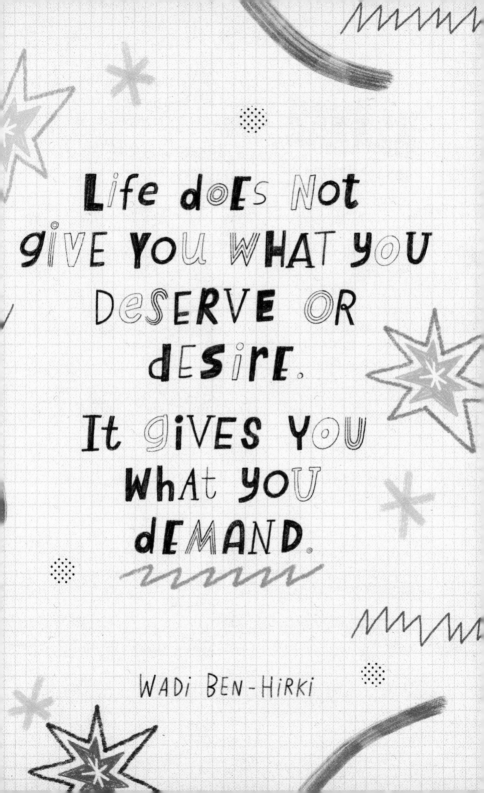

HANNAH CAMILLERI, 20

SEXUAL HARASSMENT/ASSAULT CAMPAIGNER, GIRLS AGAINST FOUNDER

Hannah Camilleri and her friends loved going to music concerts, but they didn't love the constant harassment they faced from male members of the audience. After Hannah experienced a particularly frightening situation at a gig in her hometown of Glasgow, Scotland, her friend tweeted about the incident. That tweet was noticed by a member of British band Peace, Harry Koiser, and led to Girls Against: an organisation set up by Hannah and four friends in 2015 to fight back against sexual harassment and assault at live music events.

The group started small, handing out badges at gigs across the UK. They quickly managed to get a number of British bands on board and opened up a discussion about consent, not just in the music community but in any public space. Now, they are working on talking directly to security staff, encouraging them to prevent attacks wherever possible.

Almost half of British young women have experienced unwanted sexual behaviour at music festivals. Slowly but surely, Girls Against are changing that culture. Whether it's encouraging musicians not to objectify women in their songs or giving victims a space to have their say, Hannah isn't willing to let sexual assault slip away into the shadows.

HANNAH

For my 17th birthday, I went to watch a band called Peace. I used to have a big group of friends who I'd always go to concerts with, and we ended up right at the front, just by the barrier. I was having a really good time until someone ended up behind me. Soon enough, I felt their hands on my waist. I kept subtly trying to push their hands away but they continued to keep their hands on me and started slipping them up my skirt, pinning me to the barrier with their weight.

Eventually, the crowd shifted so much that they couldn't hang on to me anymore. I continued to stand there, putting on a brave face. I remember coming home, telling my mum how good the gig was, then going straight to bed. I was in so much shock. When I did start to realise what happened, I felt almost disgusted with myself. It wasn't my first experience with sexual assault at gigs, but it was the only time I wasn't able to remove myself from the situation.

I shared my experience with a friend who then shared it on Twitter. It got a lot of reaction, including from the band itself. At the time, I was in a group chat with four other girls and we realised we'd all had similar experiences. There is a culture within music of treating women like objects. Although this is being pushed out through increased awareness, generally poor education around sex and consent doesn't help.

The next evening, we set up the Girls Against Twitter account. We didn't put much thought into it at first, but it just kept on growing. Soon, we realised we had to come up with a plan. Initially, our goal was simply to just raise awareness of the problem. But as time went on, we wanted to become more proactive and actually speak to those in the industry and work with them to make real change.

Girls Against have stalls at concerts and festivals, have given interviews to the BBC and other major news publications, and speak at universities to spread our message as much as possible. We also "employ" a few reps across the country; they provide a more focused insight in to their local area and help us have more of an even spread across the UK. We're now working with charities and are looking to achieve charitable status ourselves. We want to have a solid ground of work before we go international.

It's difficult to say whether there has been an improvement. We've definitely had less complaints sent to us online and have seen so much support. The only real resistance has come from security companies. When we've called for changes in their training, they've dismissed us as little girls and stated the issue isn't widespread enough to warrant such change.

There have also been cases of men in the music industry using their wealth to silence women, and for too long we've dismissed things as "just the way something is done." This has to change.

Although I'm planning to work in international law, particularly refugee law and war crimes, I'm going to keep up the Girls Against work. Never in a million years did I think I would be in the position I'm in now.

So, if you want to see change,
DO SOMETHING ABOUT IT.
The world really is your oyster!

MARY GRACE HENRY, 22
CHILD EDUCATION AND
SOCIAL JUSTICE CAMPAIGNER

Mary Grace Henry has always loved going to school in her hometown in Connecticut, US. So, when she learned many girls in Sub-Saharan Africa were unable to recieve an education, she wanted to help by paying for one girl to attend secondary school in Uganda. But in the end, she helped so many more.

When she was just 12, she asked her parents for a sewing machine to learn how to make hair accessories to sell at school. The first batch sold out in two days. Realising that she could keep going, Mary Grace continued sewing and selling. By the time she had finished school, she had raised enough money to fund 123 girls' schooling; to buy 286 years' worth of books, uniforms and boarding; and to fund workshops showing parents and village elders why girls deserved to be taught. She called her organisation Reverse The Course.

Mary Grace wanted to form a bond with the girls whose lives she'd changed in Kenya and Uganda, so she paid them a visit. She saw how a life of poverty could be turned into one full of financial success and ambitious ideas. She knew she could learn how to change even more lives so, at the end of 2018, she

34

made the brave decision to close her organisation and focus on her own education. When she graduates, she hopes to immerse herself in some of the deeper issues that concern us all and learn from others how to put them right.

Mary Grace isn't done with problem-solving. She's just getting started.

MARY GRACE

I went to an all-girls' Catholic school called Sacred Heart. We had a partnership with a school in Uganda and would fundraise for their students. As I got older, I started learning more about the education issues that girls face. The idea that someone couldn't attend school — not because they didn't have the money (though that was certainly an issue for many) but because they were just girls — really bothered me.

I decided to help one girl go to secondary school for four years but realised that would cost more than a typical bake sale or carwash would make. I needed to sell something that other people would want, but what? My parents made me wear hair accessories so they could keep track of me if we were walking in crowds. I loved them so figured I would make my own.

I asked my parents if I could have a sewing machine as an early birthday present. They were dubious about the idea. They understood the difficulties of running a business. But somehow, I convinced them. So we went out and found the cheapest sewing machine we could buy. I sat down in my

basement for two months, practising how to sew in a straight line, eventually managing to make 50 decent reversible headbands. Fortunately my school bookstore said yes to selling them. Within two days, all 50 had sold out. That's when everything changed.

Since then, Reverse The Course has sold over 19 thousand hair accessories and paid for 123 girls to go to school. It was really important for me to develop a meaningful connection with the girls I was supporting, despite the physical distance that separated us. So, I went to Africa to visit them and hear their incredible stories. Most of them go to boarding schools where classes start at 6 a.m. and finish at 11 p.m. But everyone was so grateful to be there; I never heard anyone complain.

Seeing this made me value my education even more. Together with my board members, I made the decision to shut down both the Reverse The Course business and foundation. This may seem like a strange thing to do but I saw three options ahead of me. I could devote 110 per cent to it but wouldn't have either the resources or skills to achieve my greater vision of helping a much bigger number of people immediately after graduating. I could keep doing 50/50. Or I could end on a high. So much of my life and identity has been tied to this social enterprise so, in a way, it feels like a part of me is ending. It's scary but exciting, because I'm going to be able to see how other people are working to change the world and learn from that. I'm planning to learn about the different problems that industries are facing throughout the world and come up with ways to solve them.

There's a lot of **FEAR** in starting
new things. But once you start,
you **LEARN DAY BY DAY**.

I'll never have all the answers, and neither will you. But education is the biggest source of empowerment in creating the change that our world is going to need. Education gives people the tools to be advocates for themselves and do the best for their communities. Education is the route to everything.

DEJA FOXX, 18
REPRODUCTIVE HEALTH CAMPAIGNER

"Why is it your right to take away my right?" Deja Foxx asked the man who refused to support a woman's right to her own body. That man was her state senator, and the video of her confrontation immediately went viral in 2017.

Deja grew up in America as a woman of colour under the wing of a single mother. She also grew up knowing what it was like to be homeless and what it was like not to have enough money to pay for the things that people would deem as essential.

But instead of accepting this inequality, she grew frustrated with how she, and many others like her, were unable to access vital services such as healthcare. That led her to team up with the organisation Planned Parenthood, and her local health centre to campaign for sexual health and birth control services to be accessible to all. But it didn't stop there; it also gave her the courage to draw attention to the existence of other big issues such as child detention facilities in Arizona and gun violence in the US.

Deja recently moved to study at Columbia University and now harbours ambitions of becoming the President of the United States so that her country can finally have a leader who represents the people. She recognises that everyone deserves the same opportunities and encourages people to fight for what should rightfully be theirs.

DEJA

When I was 11, my mum began a downward spiral into substance and alcohol abuse. This was hard but also made me mature and taught me a lot about compassion and empathy. Seeing how she struggled to get support and how I had to help provide financially enabled me to see the inequality in our society, and the ways that me and my mum were being disadvantaged. It's coloured every part of my activism.

People often think the video of me questioning senator Jeff Flake just happened. But I had been going to town halls long before that. This is where politicians meet with local people and is where I pushed members of Congress and the Senate to keep Title X (a law which gives health centres funding for birth control for low-income women) intact.

Where I live, Senator Flake is notorious for not talking to his constituents, so when he finally decided to have a town hall, I had to be there. I drove two hours and stood in line for forty-five minutes to ask that question, and was angry but unsurprised at his reaction. His response, which talked about the 'American dream', really showed the privilege he has because that 'dream', which is supposed to provide equal opportunities for any American, only rewards a very select few.

I was in high school when the video went viral. Most people thought it was cool, but some folks were hurtful. During a school debate, a group of kids made signs that said some really awful things about me. But that didn't stop me or slow me down.

I joined Planned Parenthood (PP), which is a women's and reproductive health initiative in the US. It was founded by Margaret Sanger in 1916. She was arrested several times for her political work, which included passing out pamphlets on how to prevent pregnancy during the early 1900s. Now, the organisation's services vary depending on the state, but it generally provides abortion, birth control, and STI testing. Certain communities have long had misunderstandings about the work that organisations like PP do, but now these misunderstandings are being accepted by the people in power.

I believe it's important to fight for health centres like PP, but it's also important to fight for community health centres, which are 110 per cent less controversial. I partnered with my local centre to make sure every teen in my community who wanted to take control of their reproductive health had the means to do so. We started a reproductive health access project that hires the young people we're aiming to serve, including teen mums, homeless youth, youth of colour, and independent youths like me, and we send free taxis for people who want to come to the clinic and be taught useful sex education.

Being a young person now comes with a lot of pressure. I recently started university and so many people there compared themselves to me. They thought they should be doing more. I had to remind them and myself that

this isn't a RACE;
we're NOT COMPETING with each other.
This is about all of us doing better
TOGETHER.

Students at Columbia University, where I study, tend to have a lot of wealth and privilege. They can get defensive about their backgrounds. But privilege isn't about what you've gone through, it's about what you haven't had to go through. I'm not saying that other people's lives aren't hard. But people need to recognise that their privilege allows them to be welcomed into spaces where the media will listen, so they need to be willing to pass the mic to others so that their stories can be told. They need to be active allies and ask people who are disadvantaged how they can best support them.

I don't know what I'm going to do immediately after graduating, but I do know that I'm going to run for President and I believe I'm going to win. It took me a long time to say that. But the more you say something, the more you believe what you're saying. And the more you believe it, the more others will too. For me, one of the most fundamental shifts was reminding myself that I deserve things like an Ivy League education. Now, I always say: you deserve every success you've ever had, every success you're having, and all of those yet to come.

Recognise your privilege and be willing to pass on the mic.

Deja Foxx

ARIA WATSON, 20
FEMINIST PHOTOGRAPHER

Aria Watson knows that being an activist doesn't have to involve rallies or protests. She used the power of photography to show why a man who openly disrespected women and people of colour should never be allowed to lead. Her photo series depicted semi-nude women painted with President Donald Trump's derogatory quotes about women and minorities. She called it #SignedByTrump and it went viral.

Many people supported Aria's work and yet many others rejected her – she received horrific messages, lost several friends, and argued with family members. But her determination to keep posting her photos, and her willingness to reveal herself on YouTube to all her 'haters', kept her message alive.

There's no questioning that she struggled with the publicity. She felt she had no option but to delete her social media accounts and take time away from it all. But now, she's ready to get back out there and fight for equal treatment for all. If there's one thing to take from Aria's story, it's that you cannot let others stop you, no matter how many people try.

ARIA

My life started in a really rough way. My biological mother struggled with addiction, and my biological father left when I was around one. When I was three, my grandparents thankfully decided to take me and my brother in. In my teenage years, I struggled with depression, anxiety and an eating disorder. Experiencing all of these things turned me into a very compassionate and empathetic person — and a feminist. I understand what it's like to be hurt and now my main goal is to fight for others who are struggling.

Most activists move people with their words, but my social anxiety means that's something I've never been very good at. What I am good at, however, is expressing myself in creative ways like photography.

I learned that I could mix this creativity with activism when I heard that Donald Trump was running for president. I thought it was a joke, but people in my community were supporting him. The things he said about minorities and women were disgusting, yet it seemed like some people didn't mind. I was too young to vote so I decided to make a college project about Trump.

At the time, I was living in a very conservative town, so finding someone who was willing to model semi-nude was hard. But when I told people my series was political and anti-Trump, it became even harder. A couple of models cancelled and I couldn't find someone willing to show their bare chest on camera so I had to use myself.

One of the hardest parts, however, was losing a lot of friends; they verbally attacked me online and I even had family members tell me I was going to hell. It was a painful time but I'm grateful it showed me people's true colours. The public had mixed opinions. Strangers did send me online abuse and threats, but they also showered me with so much love and support. Knowing that I had touched so many hearts encouraged me to keep speaking up.

Then Trump won the election. I was shocked, scared and angry. I couldn't believe that our country had voted for a man who'd said so many horrible things about women, people of colour, people with disabilities and I was terrified those things would become a social norm. His win pushed me to work harder and continue to post the photos, even when Instagram and Facebook deleted them because they showed a pair of breasts. If the President of the United States of America could say those things, why couldn't I post them?

Eventually, I took a break to focus on my mental health. I became insecure about my photography and felt a lot of pressure to create something that was equally as powerful. Now, I'm working on getting out there again and hope to continue to create more series that can touch others.

There is no act of activism that is too
SMALL.

I'd like to see more feminists speaking up for women in different countries. We need to fight for women in areas such as the Sudan where female genital mutilation is common, for the women in Saudi Arabia who make up just 22 per cent of the country's workforce, for the 34 million girls who don't get the opportunity to finish their primary education, and for the 830 women who die every day from preventable pregnancy-related causes.

Whatever you choose to speak up about,
don't let FEAR HOLD YOU BACK
and don't listen to those who tell you not to
do it. If you need support, you can always
REACH OUT TO ME.
I am here for you.
I BELIEVE IN YOU.

MADDY RASMUSSEN, 19

ABORTION-ACCESS CAMPAIGNER, FOUNDER OF THE SAFE PLACE PROJECT

"Anything worthwhile is worth
FIGHTING FOR."

In 26 countries around the world, women are not legally allowed to get an abortion under any circumstances. And even in countries where the procedure is legal, it can be almost impossible for some women to find a reliable and affordable clinic.

Maddy Rasmussen is seeking to change all that. When she was 16, she interned at the American women's organisation Legal Voice and had a eureka moment. The US appeared to be making it harder and harder for women to access abortion clinics, so what if there was a website providing free and easy-to-understand information? What if there was a map listing all of the country's abortion clinics?

Six months later, the Safe Place Project was born. Maddy's database lists every single abortion clinic in America. It lists the things each state requires a woman to do before they have an abortion, as well as the last date Maddy checked each clinic was open. There's even an Escape to Google button so women can keep their private life private.

Keeping the site up-to-date is Maddy's mission. Her tireless hard work has stopped women from spending days searching for a reputable place to help, or travelling for five hours only to find the clinic they were seeking had been shut down. Bearing that responsibility isn't easy but it's a burden this 19-year-old is willing to carry.

MADDY

When I was little, I was told that I could become anything I wanted when I grew up, as long as I had the ambition. But as I got older and began to have a better understanding of the world, I was surprised to see that women were rarely in positions of power. I decided I wanted to help make a difference.

My years spent at a very innovative high school called Big Picture helped cement my plans. The school swapped core classes like maths, reading, and science for project-based learning. I created the Safe Place Project map for one such project. I wanted to illustrate what abortion access looked like across the adjacent 48 states, and then realised a website would be the best outlet for the map. Nothing of its kind existed, so I knew it was important. Planned Parenthood and the National Abortion Federation had their own listings, but each only included clinics that they represented. Mine was the first to include every single clinic in one place.

Putting the list together was exhausting. There were many times where I thought it was too hard and wanted to quit. And after the 2016 presidential election, I was hesitant to release it, let alone have my name on it. But if I wasn't going to do it, who was?

All of the work ended up being totally worth it. The site showed what abortion access really looked like in the States. It's very clumped up towards the coasts (the more liberal areas of the country) and is shockingly limited in the middle.

I'm very lucky to come from one of the progressive states, but many states in the Midwest have laws and restrictions that make it difficult for women to receive abortions. These can include forcing women to have counselling before the procedure, where they can be told stories of how abortion will cause infertility and how it has links to breast cancer. Of course, none of these stories are true. They're simply used as fear tactics to scare women away. As if that wasn't enough, women can also be forced to wait anywhere from 24 to 72 hours between counselling and the actual procedure.

Funnily enough, the first article written about me was published on a notorious pro-life news site. I just laughed it off and focused on the overwhelmingly positive reaction from others. I went from reading *Teen Vogue* to being in *Teen Vogue* and received emails from people that my site has helped. It's humbling to know that what I did really mattered.

The hardest thing has been keeping the website updated. I try to do an update once a quarter but it can be difficult for me to remain on top of my college work. It's also really hard to dive back in and see that so much has changed in a matter of months.

If you want to become an activist,
EDUCATE YOURSELF.

The thing that helped me was learning as much as I could from whoever I could. I spent time researching different feminist movements and attended events where my local representatives discussed the issues they were working to push. Once you start that process, you will work out what you're interested in and can look for organisations fighting for those things.

I know I want to help the world become a better place and I want to go to law school. But what I really want is world peace so we can focus on the problems affecting our planet without war raging at the forefront of our minds.

MILLY EVANS, 19

SEX EDUCATION CAMPAIGNER

Sex ed teaches you about so many things: your body, your health, consent, as well as different sexualities and identities. Milly Evans views good sex education as a human right. But many countries disagree. In China and certain parts of the US for example, laws exist that mean children are simply taught to refrain from sex and are even given medically inaccurate information. In fact, these so-called "developed" countries are failing their youth.

Milly experienced this first-hand. Growing up in the UK, she had always talked openly about sex at home, but was disappointed to find that vital information was being withheld in her all-girls' school. But this wasn't just her school, it was a problem across the country thanks to outdated government views and some teachers' personal opinions influencing the way sex ed was taught.

So, she began raising awareness with the help of organisations such as Stonewall and the Family Planning Association. She led a school club every Thursday lunchtime, giving her classmates the chance to share their views and experiences. That led to her very own platform: I Support Sex Education. It showcases sex ed resources and gives everyone a voice, including LGBTQ+ individuals, those who have disabilities, and those who belong to ethnic minorities. Basically, anyone who feels invisible in the current UK curriculum.

But Milly doesn't just want to change the UK's way of doing things. She wants governments everywhere to promote inclusive and useful sex and relationships information, and to encourage parents to do the same at home. Sex-related curriculums can currently stagnate for 20 years before receiving any kind of update, and even then they remain old-fashioned. Milly is making sure that this will no longer be deemed acceptable.

MILLY

The world we are growing up in is so sex focused, yet young people are going out in to the world without having any tools to deal with that. Even some rural communities in Africa are far more progressive than places like the UK, especially with regard to teaching about controversial subjects such as female genital mutilation. Teaching this kind of sex education could save the government and ourselves a lot of money, energy and upset.

Sex education is crucial and fortunately has recently been made statutory in England, which means that, in 2020, it will have to be taught in schools. But even this new curriculum isn't inclusive or sex-positive. There's no focus on human rights and barely anything on LGBTQ+ relationships. The government lets teachers decide whether and how they teach something and gives parents an opt-out clause, which lets them choose whether their child receives this education until they turn 15. The worst part is that this unacceptable curriculum probably won't be updated for at least a decade.

We all deserve to have
HAPPY and HEALTHY experiences
with other people.
WE DESERVE RESPECT.

Through the Family Planning Association youth council, I campaigned in Parliament and, in 2017, I decided I wanted to change things in my school. Girls there didn't have anywhere to discuss social issues and sex ed, so I set up an activist group. It progressed to an online platform for young people across the world to write about political and social issues. Unfortunately, the website doesn't exist anymore due to lack of funding, but the idea behind it is still very much there. It's something I'd like to bring back in the future.

I went on to create I Support Sex Education because young people were all shouting the same things but weren't being heard. The goal of my campaign is to get the public, policymakers, and charities on board with sex ed as a human rights issue. To help people understand that it covers basic issues of respect and consent and is about way more than putting a condom on a banana.

My family and the other people who are really interested in the site have been amazing, but the reaction from others has been mixed. Teachers would praise and encourage me and then tell me to pipe down, so they could focus on other things, and even some of my friends found my work annoying. But more and more people are slowly getting on board.

Campaigning is extremely emotionally draining. Being able to take a break is super important because you can't make change if you're constantly exhausted. But try to stay motivated, go to as many events, and meet as many new people as you can. You just have to keep going, no matter what people say.

In an ideal world, I'd love to see sex ed incorporated in human rights law and all governments to focus on sexual and reproductive health. That would result in huge drops in poverty and violence against girls and women, and a huge drop in the mental health issues of, and violence against, the LGBTQ+ community. It would improve so many problems.

Look around you. Do you notice people that are like you? You might not have considered it before but in everyday life it's important that you see people who are similar to you and represent your values – whether that be on TV, in films or even in the job you dream of getting. If you don't, it's easy to feel alienated and think you don't belong.

For example, you could be a young black woman walking into an office full of white male faces and start to question whether you're welcome in that workplace. Or you could have a disability and see zero people like you in the media, which could make you feel different and ostracised. Or you could strive to be a model or actor but think it impossible because there's no one of your body shape and size on the catwalk or silver screen.

Fifteen per cent of the world's population has some kind of disability. They are capable and entitled to the same quality of life as anyone else. And they, along with many other overlooked communities, are fed up with the lack of representation across the board. But the attitudes of certain parts of society can often hold those with disabilities back, preventing them from reaching adulthood with a full education and lots of job opportunities on the horizon.

The following few young women are asking important questions in ever more creative ways. Why is one person deemed to be more acceptable than another? Why does size and skin colour matter so much? And why does the world urge us to conform, rather than embrace what makes us unique, from our clothes size and skin conditions to our physical appearance and personality?

They're emphasising several points. Firstly, that black, Asian and other ethnic minority individuals should be represented in our media. Secondly, that a person with a disability is entitled to a chance to flourish and access everything able-bodied people often take for granted each day. And finally, that everyone deserves to be seen and heard.

A world that looks identical is bland and boring. But it's also not realistic. True diversity isn't going to happen overnight, but we do have to start somewhere. The following women are doing all they can to resist the status quo. But they cannot do it alone. They need all of us to join them in the battle for equal representation ...

NAWAAL AKRAM, 20
COMEDIAN, MODEL, DISABILITY ADVOCATE

Nawaal Akram was diagnosed with a genetic disorder called Duchenne muscular dystrophy at the age of six. She endured four years of being bullied for the way she walked and complaints from people who thought her condition was contagious. One day, Nawaal turned up at school in Qatar to be told she was no longer welcome. Her parents desperately tried to find another school but were rejected each and every time.

When Nawaal was 12, she broke her leg, which meant she had to use a wheelchair for life. She had already lost contact with many of her friends, but this proved to be the final straw. She sank into depression and only began to embrace the wider world again when she started volunteering with Mada — a disability organisation in Qatar.

Humour became her weapon. People were unsure how to take her stand-up comedy performances at first, but she quickly gained a loyal audience. Eventually, fashion designers came calling, transforming her into Qatar's first disabled model. Now 20, Nawaal runs her own support group – Muscular Dystrophy Qatar, has a YouTube channel promoting wheelchair accessibility in her city, and has spoken about her journey on a TEDx stage.

She dreams of featuring on the cover of *Vogue Arabia*. It's only a matter of time before that becomes a reality.

NAWAAL

For me, it's an achievement to see myself doing the things I'm doing right now. Where I lived, Arabic schools accommodated people with disabilities as much as they could, but I didn't speak Arabic at the time so I studied in an international school and even some of the staff there made fun of the way I walked. Back then, people like me weren't "shown" in public in Qatar and were sometimes frowned upon or pitied.

Now, people are more accepting of disabilities, but only really if you're a disabled man. In my opinion it's much harder if you're a disabled woman, as you still face fewer employment and social opportunities. When I first went into a wheelchair, I was very young and became angry at the way society acted towards people with disabilities. But I came to understand why we faced certain struggles. I left my anger behind, learned to love people again, and embarked on a mission to change people's perceptions.

I first got involved in activism because I wanted to raise awareness of my (and others') lack of schooling. I thought all my work would help me get that education. Unfortunately, it didn't but it did get me recognised.

I started with comedy. I'd been watching a comedic group called Stand Up Comedy Qatar since 2012, and wanted to perform, but was initially too scared. I thought people might think they were laughing at me, rather than with me. It was my mum who finally convinced me to go on stage. Yes, people were afraid to laugh but I told them it was okay. The performances kept happening and

I officially became Qatar's
FIRST STAND-UP COMEDIAN
who can't stand up!

I also became a model. My comedy had spread throughout Qatar and caught the attention of a Qatari brand. They asked me to model for them – wheelchair included. Then more brands came and approached me too.

There's a thinking all around the world that if you have a disability, you're socially challenged. But I know a lot of people with physical disabilities that have a much better social life than people who don't. So, my work is also trying to break this stigma and show that wheelchairs are an aid to help you move around, not an obstacle.

It's also true that people with disabilities are often not represented in the media, whether it's in films, adverts or fashion shows. Movies for example often show disabled people as characters that want to die or who struggle to be loved. They don't show our friendships, the outfits we decide to wear each day, or even our issues with our wheelchairs. And this problem isn't just in the Middle East either. It's in the UK, it's in Asia, it's worldwide.

I'm therefore determined to leave a mark in history. I'm creating a path for future generations and other girls with disabilities so they can see there is someone like them modelling, there is someone like them doing comedy, there is someone like them in the media. If I can do it, they can do it too. But to make a change, you have to learn to accept yourself too. At first, I didn't want to talk about my disease, but once I accepted it, I was able to campaign for my rights.

Being an activist does require focus too. I made a to-do list of the people I wanted to meet and the things I wanted to achieve. And then I did them one by one. You have to believe in yourself.

MILLICENT SIMMONDS, 15

ACTRESS

Millicent "Millie" Simmonds is deaf. But that doesn't define her. Losing her hearing as a baby meant she has known little else and has never felt held back. But she will admit that seeing a lack of people with hearing difficulties (or any difficulties for that matter) in the media convinced her that it wasn't possible to enter the limelight.

Still, she didn't give up hope. When she was 13, she got her big break in the drama *Wonderstruck*. Millie's performance as a defiant deaf girl in the 1920s earned her several award nominations. Then *A Quiet Place* was released. Billed as one of the most exciting horror films in decades, Millie wowed audiences in cinemas as well as her fellow actors on set.

Millie stresses how important it is for people to learn sign language, whether it's to communicate with a deaf colleague, friend or even family member. She has experienced nothing but praise for this activism, but she realises that one person isn't going to make all of the changes that are needed in the world either.

So, she wants to see people from all walks of life – not just the deaf community – involved in telling their stories. Because the more stories we hear, the more compassion we have, and that is something we really need right now and in the years to come.

MILLICENT

When my mum found out I was deaf, she immediately started learning sign language and taught my two brothers. I started communicating with them when I was six months old, so home was fairly easy for me. But there were times when I didn't understand what was going on. If someone wasn't interpreting for me, I was lost.

I wish people understood how
ALONE and ISOLATED
deaf people can feel.

I've felt left out in some way, every day, my whole life. If people could just learn a few signs like, "Hi, how are you? Good to see you," it really would go a long way.

Most of my family, however, didn't want to learn. Dealing with and accepting that fact was hard because people who can hear can learn sign language easier than deaf people can learn to speak. If you want to communicate with someone who is deaf, 100 per cent of the responsibility is on you. We can't meet you halfway.

I loved interacting with kids that were like me, so loved going to a deaf school. But sometimes, that was hard too. I had a cochlear implant and grew up in a hearing family so some of the kids made fun of me for not being "deaf enough".

I don't remember learning how to act; it just came naturally to me. As a kid, I was very observant. I would always act out stories at school and, at home, would impersonate the way people walked or acted to try and make my family laugh.

My teacher asked me to join the drama club when I was very young. My first real performance was for a deaf conference in Utah when I was around seven or eight. There were probably a hundred people watching me play Puck in *A Midsummer Night's Dream*. I don't remember being nervous at all but, looking back now, I probably should have been!

My recent acting experience still feels like a dream. I don't know how else to describe it, other than incredible. The people I've met and the friendships I've made have to be my favourite parts. I love to act and work, but I love the bonds that I have with other people more than anything. I'm so grateful to the ones who put effort in to learning how to communicate with me.

It's sad when people who can hear are cast for deaf roles. There are so many talented deaf actors out there that deserve those opportunities. Our stories and experiences are just as important; our stories need to be told. And we don't just need more deaf actors. We need deaf directors, deaf producers, and deaf writers too.

I hope I haven't had my greatest achievement yet. I'm still so young and would love to keep acting for as long as I can because it brings me joy. My dream role would be a villain — I don't think anyone would ever suspect me! I also really want to travel and would love to move to New York. The city is so diverse. No one stares at me when they see me signing there. I feel like I fit in. I feel like I belong.

KADEEJA KHAN, 22

BEAUTY BLOGGER, SKIN POSITIVITY CAMPAIGNER

Getting spots is almost a rite of passage for any young person – you can blame those pesky hormones! But the beauty industry and advertising rarely flaunt anything other than clear "flawless" skin. And Kadeeja Khan has had enough.

Kadeeja has had acne from the age of 12. She has been bullied for the way her skin looked and was diagnosed with depression. She found that make-up was her way out of the darkness, so began posting carefully edited selfies on Instagram. Eventually, she found the courage to post pictures of her natural self.

As her following grew, brands began reaching out. When an agency asked Kadeeja to star in a new L'Oreal advert, she was over the moon. Finally, the beauty industry was ready to show women as they actually were. Unfortunately, her happiness was short lived. A few days later, she was told her "skin issues" meant she couldn't be in the campaign. Kadeeja wanted people to know, so she posted the email on social media.

That post went viral, resulting in several apologies from both the agency and L'Oreal who said she had been mistakenly booked for a hair-dye advert, not a skincare one and that they do work with women and men with all skin types, celebrating diversity. But Kadeeja had found a new path. She used her public profile to share her experience of acne, to show other young people how to cover up their spots if they wanted to, and, most vitally, to prove that beauty comes in more than one form.

Kadeeja asks everyone to love their unedited selves. Because when an industry that profits from making us feel bad about ourselves loses its power over us, it will be them who has to take a good hard look in the mirror.

KADEEJA

In school, people used to make fun of me. They would call me "pizza face" and tell me to clean my skin. I hated looking at myself and thought my life would be different if I didn't have acne. I thought I'd be able to have friends and be in the popular group at school.

When I put make-up on, I felt like that person. Blogging about beauty allowed me to get away from the reality of not feeling beautiful. I wanted to share my experience so people who had lived in my shoes would know they weren't alone, but one day woke up feeling angry and frustrated because I wasn't living my life as myself.

I didn't want to spend any more time pretending to be flawless, so I ditched the Photoshop. It didn't happen overnight; it was a very long process. But when I finally showed the online world my skin, I experienced so much bullying. Comments were flowing, flowing, flowing. People were telling me I was ugly and disgusting. I was embarrassed and couldn't believe that that was what people thought of me. So I edited and posted a second photo and tried to backpedal before thinking to myself, "I don't care how many people say nasty things, I'm not going to give in."

The bullying still comes today. People on the internet can blast you with your worst fears and insecurities, forcing you to mould into this tough character. I've been told to accept the comments because I'm on a social platform, but sometimes it's not that easy.

 We're all **HUMAN** and we all have **FEELINGS**.

When L'Oreal gave me an opportunity and took it away, I broke down. I couldn't believe that a huge beauty brand that I loved would openly say it couldn't be involved with me in that particular campaign because of my skin issues. It knocked my confidence for a while, but I didn't let it break me. Instead, it encouraged me to share even more positivity.

It's sad that brands today care more about money than the young boys and girls who love their make-up. Some beauty brands put out a perfect image of how you'd look if you used their products. But the model they use in the advert has never suffered with skin problems. People are going see it and think, "If I don't look like that, then maybe there's something wrong with me." In reality, there's nothing wrong with any of us. If companies would just wake up to that, things would improve.

I don't want to be continuously surrounded by brands that don't support people of different skin types and conditions, so I'm working to change things from outside of the beauty community. I now give motivational speeches about loving yourself and aim to give people confidence.

I do believe you will get somewhere just being you. If I wasn't myself, I wouldn't be in a Rimmel London campaign with Rita Ora and Cara Delevingne or be a part of Makeup Revolution's foundation advert. Knowing that you're not putting on an act while doing something you love is the most amazing feeling.

DON'T CHANGE YOURSELF FOR ANYONE. YOU WILL GET SOMEWHERE JUST BEING YOU.

KADEEJA KHAN

JORDAN REEVES, 13

ADVOCATE FOR LIMB DIFFERENCES, "BORN JUST RIGHT" INNOVATOR

Jordan Reeves' left arm ends just below the elbow. She notices people staring. Rather than replying rudely, Jordan thought it would be better to educate the world on what it's like to have a limb difference and how you should speak to someone who's missing an arm or leg. Hint: it's just how you'd talk to anyone else.

When Jordan was little more than a baby, her mum, Jen, started a blog called Born Just Right. It has now grown into a non-profit organisation with Jordan as the main ambassador and lead innovator. She travels round the country changing attitudes, and has also become an inventor, creating both fun and useful prosthetics.

One prosthetic shoots glitter at anyone who gets in her way. Others featuring pirate hooks and hand attachments will soon follow. With the guidance of 3D experts, she is helping children to do simple things like pull off paper towels, while also enabling them to live out their comic book dreams! Marvel should take note of this young campaigner. Because if it was up to Jordan, a one-armed and one-legged Avenger would already exist.

JORDAN

For those who don't know, a limb difference is when part of a limb (finger(s), toe(s), hand(s), arm(s) and/or leg(s)) is missing. Some people are born with limb differences like me. Some people have accidents or get sick and have to have their limb amputated. I don't consider myself an amputee because I never lost anything. I was born this way.

I'm able to do everything other kids can do. Sometimes, I just do it differently. I tie my shoes and use zippers; all that snazzy stuff. When people realise I have a little arm, they react in one of many ways. Many act surprised; some are chilled. Some look like they might scream in fear; others ask questions. And some just stare. Sometimes I feel embarrassed and don't want to explain. But growing up around people who didn't have disabilities made it easy for me to see that I could educate a lot of people if I spoke up.

I get nervous before doing any big speech. I've never felt worried about what I'm going to say, I just worry I will mess up saying it! But

MY NORMAL isn't
EVERYONE'S NORMAL,

and I think it's important to explain what that means.

Born Just Right launched when I was younger. My mum realised that I was just as involved in getting it started as she was, so now I'm listed as the cofounder. Kids with disabilities have to do things differently. We have to come up with solutions by ourselves and therefore naturally know what makes a good design. The Born Just Right organisation teaches them even more about it and shows them exactly how to build on their differences.

Project Unicorn is the most famous prosthetic that I've designed. I went to a design camp for kids with limb differences and was asked what my special power would be if I was a superhero. I decided I wanted to shoot glitter! I came up with a few different prototypes then worked with a design partner to turn my idea into a unicorn horn prosthetic that shoots biodegradable glitter.

This gave me a chance to show how a disability isn't sad, but a chance to do something fun instead. After all, a two-handed person can't shoot from a glitter-filled prosthetic! I still wish upper arm prosthetics were more comfortable and not so clunky, so I'm continuing to tinker. Maybe one of my other ideas will become a reality one day.

I'm also working on getting more mainstream toys to show limb differences. When I was four, my mum bought me an American Girl doll that had the same outfit as me. She said it looked just like me, but I was confused by that because the doll had two hands. So, at the end of 2015, I started a Change.org petition asking doll manufacturer American Girl to consider offering limb difference options. The petition now has 26,000 signatures.

In the future, I want to make sure people with disabilities are included in both big and small decisions in society. A person who looks or acts differently isn't scary; they're simply a person who sees the world in a different way.

MC SOFFIA, 15

RAPPER

Soffia Gomes da Rocha Gregório Correa (or MC Soffia as she's more commonly known) is a Brazilian rapper who raps to remind people about her country's racist attitudes. Soffia experienced racism at an extremely young age. When she was in kindergarten, a classmate told her that her skin was black because she fell into a tin of paint, so Soffia went home and told her mum that she wanted to be white. It was at this point that her mother and grandmother taught her all about racism.

Soffia's mum was a known figure in Brazil's hip-hop movement. She took her to workshops so that she could learn more about her roots. There, Soffia reclaimed her identity. She wrote her first song at nine. Her lyrics instantly formed battle songs, inspiring women of colour everywhere. One track, 'Menina Pretinha', includes the memorable lines: "I'm black and proud of my colour ... My hair is dope, it doesn't need a flat iron."

Her refreshing honesty earned her an invite to the opening ceremony stage of the 2016 Olympic Games. Representing Brazil – the world's largest black population outside of Africa – she performed with millions of people watching and invited all minorities to celebrate their cultures too. There is still a long way to go until racism becomes a thing of the past in Brazil and in the wider world, but Soffia is hopeful that the future is a more colourful one.

SOFFIA

Being born black is very difficult in any country. So is being born a woman. But I don't talk about the pain or curse racist people in my songs. I talk about acceptance because we have to accept ourselves and everyone else just has to have respect.

My family have always told me that I was beautiful, but they also told me to remember that people would criticise me for my hair. Yet when I actually experienced racism for the first time, I was still in shock. I realised that racism really was real.

I've been interested in hip-hop since I was six. My mother took me to a project called Future of Hip-Hop where I learned how to graffiti, breakdance, DJ and MC. My mother has always given me strength and showed me I could be whatever I wanted. She will always be there by my side helping me.

When I was nine, I wrote my first song with my grandmother. All of my songs are a way of supporting the current generation and are equally important. However, one of my favourites is called *Menina Pretinha*. It was the one that made me grow up and showed me that there were many other girls in the same fight. Another favourite is *Barbie Black*. The lyrics are about not following the tall, skinny and blonde standards of beauty.

We have to understand and accept that there are **DIFFERENT** types of bodies. We have to show **EQUALITY**.

80

Change also needs to happen in schools. The classroom is where children spend a lot of their time and is where we should be being taught important issues. By talking about the existence of black people and the reason why our hair looks the way it does, about how women's bodies work, about why girls menstruate, and about why we should respect everyone's differences, we can prevent malicious actions like racism and bullying. No one has the right to commit any of these acts and no one deserves to go through them.

I have a lot of new music that requires a sponsor and producer. But I'm taking a music production class so that I can produce my own songs. I intend to conquer a new dream of mine every hour of every day and try to believe that nothing is impossible. For example, I believe that I *will* sing alongside Beyoncé one day. I'm just waiting for her call.

My work has already helped people. They listen to me and realise the importance of a black girl's voice. Young people who too want to make a difference should never try to act like another person.

Be different. Run after your DREAMS
and seek SUPPORT in your families.

Know the history of your skin and go after your stories.

MADELINE STUART, 22

MODEL, DIVERSITY AND DISABILITY ADVOCATE

One day, Madeline Stuart uttered three simple words to her mum: "Mum, me model." She knew that the fashion industry had a narrow view of what a model should look like. She knew someone like her, someone with Down syndrome, wasn't likely to fit that view.

But that didn't stop Madeline from achieving her goal of making the fashion world a more inclusive place. Having three holes in her heart encouraged her to focus on improving her health. After losing a lot of weight in order to do this, she took to social media to encourage others to think about their health too. That one viral post led to the thing she'd been dreaming of: an invitation to model for a fashion brand.

She has since become the first person with Down syndrome to model at London, Paris and New York Fashion Week. She has modelled in over 100 fashion shows, travelling across the world from her native Australia to places such as Russia, China and Uganda. She has appeared in a Diesel campaign, been named the ambassador for P&O Cruises, and featured on the pages of newspapers and magazines such as the *New York Times* and *Vogue*. And her push for diversity is finally working!

Madeline has also started to design clothes. In 2017, she launched her own clothing line, 21 Reasons Why, at New York Fashion Week. However, she still wants to conquer more as a model. She aims to walk for bigger and bigger brands each year, eventually landing on the catwalks of Chanel, Louis Vuitton and Victoria's Secret.

At 22 years old, Madeline has already inspired millions of people, proving that she really is a powerful force to be reckoned with.

The following was written by Madeline and her mother Rosanne Stuart.

MADELINE

I've had an amazing life with my mum; she never held me back and always treated me like I didn't have a disability. In fact, she and my grandparents were my main support network when I was growing up.

I fell in love with modelling when my mum took me to a fashion show in Brisbane. I watched the models on the catwalk having so much fun and looking so confident and beautiful. I knew I wanted to have a go. I was never scared, only excited. I knew how much I would love it and it turns out I was right! I can't get enough of modelling now.

The first time I modelled professionally was my first season of New York Fashion Week. It all happened so quickly. A company that had teamed up with a designer called Hendrik

Vermeulen and a paralysis charity called the Christopher Reeve Foundation called me. After doing some research, my mum and I agreed this was a great platform. We believed in both the foundation and the designer's work. His line was about saving the oceans and my first dress was made out of recycled plastic.

Walking in that show was an amazing experience. I was excited because I was about to walk in one of the biggest fashion events in the world and proud of how hard I had worked to get there. As well as New York, I've also loved walking in fashion shows in Paris and London. My job means I've been fortunate enough to travel the world and I love that I've been able to see so many beautiful places.

The reaction from people in the fashion industry towards me has been mostly positive, which is something that I'm very thankful for. But I did experience one problem. Some people didn't see me as a professional model, and occasionally expected me to model for free. It was disheartening to see people treating me in this way. But anything worthwhile is worth fighting for, so I worked to educate people and am happy to say that I am finally being treated in the same way as all of the other models.

People had always commented on my sense of style and I was looking to find something that would represent me, so starting my own clothing line, 21 Reasons Why, just seemed right. Every part of its name means something to me. The number 21 signifies two things: the extra 21st chromosome that results in Down syndrome, and the fact that everyone looks forward to turning 21. The second part of the name stands for all the reasons I believe we can be kinder and more loving and inclusive. Designing is a really fun process and I'm currently looking for an investor to take my clothes to stores around the world.

It's so encouraging to see the changes that are being made within the fashion industry. But I do think it still has a long way to go. The road to get to where I am now is still significantly more difficult for those with disabilities. I want that to change and will continue to work hard to see more diversity and inclusion in the industry. I would love to see someone with a disability be the face of a brand. That would really break down the barriers.

Believe in yourself and never give up on your dreams. Remember that rejection will only make you stronger and push you to prove people wrong. I hope I am proof that hard work and determination will get you exactly where you want to go.

Anything worthwhile is worth fighting for.

MADELINE STUART

HOLLY JACOBSON, 16

FILMMAKER AND ACTRESS

Holly Jacobson has seen two sides of the camera: what goes on in front of it and what occurs hidden way behind the scenes. As a young actress, she grew tired of the stereotypical ways in which girls and women were shown on screen. She set out to write her own stories and, at the age of nine, released her very first film.

Her passion for powerful storytelling has earned her several glittering awards. More importantly, it has shown that three-dimensional female characters with realistic personalities and strong opinions are well worth watching.

Now 16, Holly has just wrapped up making and directing her biggest venture yet: a truly modern retelling of *Hansel and Gretel*. She raised thousands of pounds and took charge of a huge crew, not even letting something as disastrous as a fire on set stop her from executing her vision.

After a major Hollywood movie casting forced her, and countless other young girls, to wait for eight hours in the searing heat, Holly also saw first-hand how her industry often seeks to promote itself rather than the wellbeing of the people it hires. She therefore aims to highlight that everyone, particularly child actors, should be treated fairly in the industry.

And she isn't afraid to speak her mind about the failings of her industry and encourages girls and women to take control of their own stories and destinies. Her message? Change is coming to the film industry. Change that will see a new representation of women, on and off screen.

HOLLY

My first acting job happened by accident. A family friend who worked in film had booked a child actor for a series of short films. The original girl fell ill so I was asked to step in. The adult actors on set encouraged me to start acting professionally. I was only six.

I went on to act in several short indie films, developing an interest in photography, SFX make-up, and, of course, filmmaking. I loved acting and still do but being a child actor means being a tool for someone else's story. I wanted to have stories that were in my head be on the screen too.

Although I initially didn't have the technical skill set to make films, I realised this didn't have to be a roadblock as films are made by way more than one person. All I needed to do was find other people who could help. So, when I was nine, I made my first film for a local competition and won, jumping straight into my next project. I had difficulty asserting myself on set as I was completely inexperienced. But the more projects that I worked on, the more skills I learned.

After I turned 13, I decided the time was right to create a film that I'd been wanting to make for four years. The fairy tale *Hansel and Gretel* has always seemed odd to me. In the traditional story, the father takes his two kids into the forest and leaves them there to die on the advice of their "evil" stepmother. In the end, the children make it home, the stepmother is gone, and everyone lives happily ever after. But this was odd to me – their dad quickly got on board with child murder, yet it was the woman who was blamed! Women are seriously blamed for everything.

I knew this film, which I called *Harry and Grace*, would be a major undertaking. I managed to save £2,000 on my own but needed more, so I started a crowdfunding campaign to raise another few thousand. We had to build a major set in the middle of the woods and had volunteers living there for months. My crew often exceeded 30 people, and there was even a crowd scene with more than 70 extras. All of that work means I can't bear for it to be less than perfect. I'm home-schooled, so I have a lot more time to spend perfecting things, but that also forces me to constantly push myself.

It hurts to see how girls and women's lives are secondary to men's in film. Men are written as full and rounded characters, while women have the same tired old stereotypes trotted out again and again. Here's a clue for any would-be writer: a girl can be pretty without being nasty and a girl can also be blonde without being an airhead.

> I'd advise anyone who doesn't like the status quo to vote with their cash.

AND DON'T WATCH FILMS THAT SIDELINE WOMEN.

As well as more realistic characters, I'd like to see a more diverse film industry, both on camera and behind it. More women, more racial diversity, more representation of people with disabilities, and more well-rounded gay, bi, and trans characters. On film sets, I do at least see women directing but men often interrupt and undermine them, even to the point of taking over and giving different direction to the actors.

The biggest gender difference I see on sets, however, is that men will say they can do a job when they only know a little about it, while women will only say they can do something when they're pretty much perfect at it. This is why so many female photography students give up possession of the camera. Girls, have confidence in yourselves. It's okay to be assertive and insist on being heard. We need to be one another's allies, so don't look at other young women as your competition. This is a new generation of filmmakers and I believe the future is equal.

DIANA SIROKAI, 22
BODY-POSITIVE MODEL

Diana Sirokai spent her early childhood in Hungary hating the way she looked. But when she moved to London, she realised the "ideal" body shape just didn't exist and so she joined the fashion industry as a curve model. Yet even then some people bullied her for being "too big" to model, so she ploughed all her frustrations in to creating a body-positive community on Instagram. Her account now has over 700 thousand followers who seek out Diana's encouraging words each and every day.

She posts photos of herself wearing clothes that plus-size women are typically told not to. She recreates fashion adverts, showing brands why they should be showcasing more than one body type. She writes fierce captions to accompany her equally powerful images.

One of her posts compares an unedited bikini photo with the Photoshopped version. The caption reads: "Do you ever feel the need to look perfect for social media, beach or life in general? What does looking good mean exactly? ... How many companies would stop making money if women today decided to love their appearance? All of them!"

Diana is no ordinary influencer. She is using her status to alter the course of history so that, in years to come, we can all pick up a fashion magazine and not be surprised at the diverse people of all shapes and sizes staring straight back.

DIANA

My relationship with my body has never been like it is now. I used to hate the way I looked because people in Hungary always told me I was fat. But when my mum and I moved to London, I experienced the complete opposite reaction. Instead of telling me to lose weight, people there seemed to love a little meat.

I ended up getting so much attention on the street that I had anxiety from the age of 13. We then lived in Tenerife for two years and only moved back to London when I told my mum I wanted to be a model.

I started modelling but was bullied for being a "fat" model, so I quit the industry. One day, I looked in the mirror and remembered all the hate and tears I had gone through. I decided to never go back to that feeling.

As soon as I decided to stop hating myself, I felt the strength to return to modelling and show women that they could love themselves. I used to look at fashion adverts and think that I could never look that good. But when I gained this confidence, I looked at those campaigns differently.

I knew that a plus-size model could look just as good as a "regular" model, so why weren't they being shown? I realised that everyone needs someone to relate to and knew I could be that person for the plus-size community. I put myself in those campaigns to send a body-positive message. I didn't expect my photos to go viral but seeing such a strong reaction convinced me to keep going.

Now, I have so many Instagram followers. I've learned that

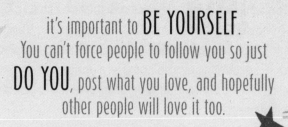

it's important to **BE YOURSELF**.
You can't force people to follow you so just
DO YOU, post what you love, and hopefully
other people will love it too.

I always thought modelling in Hungary would be my biggest challenge. I grew up there and know that the country isn't as open-minded about things like plus-size models. But I ended up being published in *Glamour Hungary* magazine. To see that I have a voice in my home and am able to inspire so many girls is insane.

The fashion industry is definitely changing, but it's not changing enough. It now accepts the fact that plus-size women slay too but it still doesn't seem to realise that there are a lot of different identities in this world. The industry needs to start using all kinds of models: petite, plus, and models of all ethnicities. We live in such a diverse world. Fashion isn't just for one kind of person.

Eventually, I want to stop recreating adverts that other models appear in and finally star in my own campaign with a high fashion brand. I want to see more people standing up for each other and I want to see more positivity because, sometimes, a smile is all it takes to make someone's day.

Whatever you decided to do with your life, don't give up. If I gave up, you wouldn't be reading my story today. I want to read yours.

MARIA OSADO, 21

FOUNDER OF GÜERXS MODELLING AGENCY

Maria Osado has always been interested in fashion, but it wasn't until she reached her teenage years that she noticed something strange about the industry. Magazines in her native Mexico were holding white people up as the ultimate beauty ideal. She wondered why the 65 per cent of Mexicans with brown or black skin weren't being shown.

Maria's friends felt the same. She knew they weren't the only ones, so in 2016, she started Güerxs; a modelling agency with one big difference. Her models aren't necessarily tall and thin and are definitely not all white. A lot don't even bend to conventional gender stereotypes. Instead, they are 100 per cent unique.

The entire name of her agency reminds Maria what she has set out to do. "Güero" is a slang word for someone with what we recognise as typical European features – think fair skin, blonde hair, and blue eyes. The "x" meanwhile banishes the traditional "as" or "os" gender rules of the Spanish language, further pushing her non-binary message.

Maria also wants the world to see the real Mexico. She knows it's more than how other countries view it, which is either a jolly tourist destination or a place plagued by violence and drugs. So, she enlists artists, campaigners, dancers, and students who embody the reality she sees every day.

Maria wants to broaden her horizons and represent Mexicans living all over the world. Because no one but you can, and should, represent your community.

MARIA

Growing up in Mexico was a huge lesson for me and many other young people. If you are awake to what is going on, you are constantly learning. This is because Mexico is a country with huge contrasts; both good and bad.

The good side comes from the varied and rich culture. The bad side is the huge difference between wealthy people and the rest of the population who are struggling and have few opportunities. You can see this gap when you walk around. Some areas have had a lot of money invested in them to appeal to tourists. But if you walk two blocks, you'll find areas that are the complete opposite.

I've always loved experimenting with my clothes. But when I was 15, I started to notice that the fashion industry was creating a parallel universe that had nothing to do with the world I was living in. Magazine covers were mostly featuring white people, and I couldn't see anyone on the streets of Mexico who could relate to the people in the advertising campaigns. It took some sleepovers with my friends to figure out that there needed to be a change and that that change could come from me.

I wanted to challenge beauty standards and start a platform to showcase the diversity that I thought Mexico, and the world, needed to see. So, when I was 18, I started the agency with nothing but a manifesto and an instant camera.

In a way, Güerxs is like my biography. The models I scout come from the different parts of my life. Some of them belong to the high school I used to go to and some are just people I've found through the location settings on Instagram. That platform in itself is another way of breaking the boundaries that fashion has created.

Right now, the agency has 20 models. My first approach was to focus on just Mexico but now I want to speak to a bigger audience. That means representing young Mexicans living in Latin America, third world countries, and the US.

The one thing people and brands need to remember is that

DIVERSITY IS NOT A MARKETING TOOL.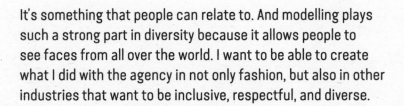

It's something that people can relate to. And modelling plays such a strong part in diversity because it allows people to see faces from all over the world. I want to be able to create what I did with the agency in not only fashion, but also in other industries that want to be inclusive, respectful, and diverse.

As a generation, we're definitely taking steps forward. In Mexico, I've seen some things improve and some things get harder. But at least there is always hope.

ENVIRONMENT

Something odd has happened. You see, a long time ago we were much more reluctant to waste anything. Having a roof over our heads and the ability to eat three meals a day was considered a luxury. But somehow, things started to change. We began wasting resources, buying things we didn't really need, and mindlessly throwing them away when we quickly became bored.

This greed inflicted heavy damage on the thing that has kept every generation of humans alive: Earth. Scientists have been trying to warn us for years that drastic action needs to be taken but we haven't been listening.

Yet groups of young people are now spreading important messages of sustainability and survival. They're telling everyone to cut back on their unnecessary use of plastics, to stop destroying animals' natural habitats, and to take a good hard look at how their everyday lifestyles are impacting the future.

We have already had a glimpse of that impact. Air pollution is responsible for the deaths of seven million people a year. Experts predict that, by 2050, there will be more plastic in the ocean than fish. And 60 per cent of the world's animals have vanished in less than 50 years thanks to humans. If you put that in people terms, that's roughly the populations of Africa, Europe, North America,

South America, China and Oceania combined.

All of those statistics are horrifying to think about, but we mustn't bury our heads in the sand. Together, we can save the planet! We can raise awareness of what's really happening and show people how to make a difference. We can stop global temperatures from increasing, reduce the number of catastrophic natural disasters, and transform Earth back in to a safe and healthy home.

Nature is the reason we're still here, and the following campaigners will show you it's our responsibility to repay that debt.

ISABEL AND MELATI WIJSEN, 16 AND 18

BYE BYE PLASTIC BAGS COFOUNDERS,
ENVIRONMENTALISTS AND YOUNG CHANGEMAKERS

The Wijsen sisters grew up in what most of us would call paradise. But the beautiful Indonesian island of Bali has a saddening downside. Tonnes of plastic rubbish pollute the ocean, ending up on its pristine beaches.

Plastic first became popular in the home in the 1960s and is now a huge part of our lives. But most of the plastic items we buy (bottles, bags and cotton buds) are single-use, which means we use them once and throw them away. The problem is that this plastic can take hundreds of years to break down, turning into smaller and smaller pieces along the way. Much of this microplastic ends up in the ocean, joining bigger pieces that animals can fatally mistake for food. Even the fish that we eat may contain tiny forms of plastic.

The pollution in Bali has become such a problem that the rainy months are now known as "trash season". When Isabel was ten and Melati turned 12, they decided they could no longer ignore the problem. Inspired by global leaders such as Nelson Mandela and Princess Diana, they started Bye Bye Plastic Bags: an organisation that aims to do exactly what its name suggests.

The siblings thought they needed Bali's governor on their side, so they set up a petition. It received over 100 thousand signatures; a significant achievement for an island that has just over four million people living on it. Unfortunately, their governor still wouldn't meet them. So, they went one step further, going on a controlled food strike. Two days later, the governor ushered them into his office and gave them a signed letter stating that he would help make Bali plastic bag free. But years passed with little sign of government action. The Wijsens weren't deterred. They alone organised the biggest beach clean-up Bali has ever seen, were recognised by both *Time* magazine and CNN, and grew Bye Bye Plastic Bags in to a global youth-led organisation that now exists in over 30 countries across the planet.

And Bali's government? Well, it's finally listened to those cries for change ...

ISABEL AND MELATI

Growing up in Bali was magical. We were raised in a house in the middle of the rice fields, a hundred metres from the ocean. Our parents are from two different worlds, Indonesia and the Netherlands, and it felt like they had created a special one for us to grow up in. But one where climate change was also real.

When we noticed the plastic taking over Bali's beaches, we decided we had to do something. We didn't want to wait until we were older to start making a difference. We could already see the negative impact that plastic was having on our environment.

So, we started Bye Bye Plastic Bags. Our goal is to make the people living in Bali (and everywhere else) say no to single-use plastic bags. We had many meetings with the government on both a local and national level, and found that our biggest challenge was getting the government to implement the promises that it had made. Sometimes, it was like asking an elephant to dance!

Bye Bye Plastic Bags started small. But after we spoke on international stages, we received emails from youths all over the world asking how to start it in their own country. Today, Bye Bye Plastic Bags is in over 30 countries. Luckily, we have a lot of helping hands! The entire journey has been like a school of life. We've learned so much that a normal textbook could never teach us and are proud of so many things.

On a personal level, we are proud to have spoken at the United Nations in New York and to have been announced as one of the most inspirational women in Indonesia by *Forbes*. Team-wise, we are proud to have organised the biggest beach clean-up ever held in Bali. Twenty thousand people showed up and, in one single day, we collected 65 tonnes of plastic waste.

Keeping our organisation going with new ideas and strategies and keeping the team motivated is a big struggle. Our latest campaign is called KOMITMEN. We're asking companies to sign a commitment saying no to single-use items. It has been a success and is proof that the people of Bali are ready to leave the plastic industry with or without the government's help.

But finally, after five years of hard campaigning, we have the government on our side. It has set out regulations and released a statement saying that Bali's capital of Denpasar will be the start of a bag ban across the island. Now, local authorities in most parts of Bali have banned single use plastic bags!

We hope that humans become aware of how we are destroying the environment with the way that we live. But we, the youth, do not have the luxury to wait. You are never too young to stand up and speak out.

You can create **CHANGE** through **EMPOWERMENT** and **EDUCATION**.

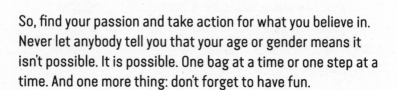

So, find your passion and take action for what you believe in. Never let anybody tell you that your age or gender means it isn't possible. It is possible. One bag at a time or one step at a time. And one more thing: don't forget to have fun.

LILLY PLATT, 10

Plastic pollution however isn't just a problem in Bali, it's worldwide. In 2015, Lilly Platt was walking to McDonald's with her grandpa. Her recent move from the UK to Holland meant she was still getting to grips with the Dutch language so, to help, her grandpa asked her to count in Dutch how many pieces of plastic she saw along the way. The total? A whopping 91 pieces.

Soon after, she began picking up plastic every time she stepped outside, posting a photo of her environmentally harmful finds on social media. Lilly's Plastic Pickup page quickly started inspiring other people around the world to recycle the rubbish left on their streets and to refuse single-use plastics.

Lilly has since travelled hundreds of miles to clean up beaches and has convinced local companies to change their plastic usage. On her tenth birthday, she even kickstarted a worldwide initiative with Lilly's Global Cleanup Day that is set to take place every April.

Changing habits is difficult, but Lilly believes that education and protest will encourage people to say no to plastic. It's safe to say that her several thousand followers agree.

LILLY

I was born in London but moved to Holland when I was six. My grandpa lives there and he inspired me to love nature even more than I already did. He knows the answer to every question in the world and helped me see the effect that plastic was having.

One day, I was walking to McDonald's with him and decided to count the amount of plastic on the floor. In an 11-minute walk, we counted 91 pieces. Grandpa then told me that any piece of litter dropped on the floor would somehow make its way to the ocean. It might take a day, a week, a month, or even a year but it will end up there.

I started Lilly's Plastic Pickup to help people see how much plastic is out there. I walk around, pick up rubbish, and then sort it in to categories such as glass, cans and plastic bags. Then I take a photo of everything I've found and put it on social media. Local and national news came and took photos of my early pick ups. Then I received a call from an organisation called Plastic Pollution Coalition. They told me about the four Rs: Recycle, Reuse, Renew, and Refuse.

I wanted to help people refuse single-use plastic, so I teamed up with my friends at Your Straw to make a reusable bag that contains a bamboo spork, bamboo straws and a straw cleaner. Straws are one of our biggest enemies in the plastic pollution fight, but you can stop using them by taking this set with you wherever you go. I've given them to lots of people: The Prime Minister of Curaçao and conservationist Jane Goodall being some of the most famous.

I also travel to help clean up other places. In Norway, there is an island where the first thing you see is all of the microplastic that occurs when plastic is left somewhere for a really long time and breaks up in to small pieces. It was very difficult to pick up the millions of tiny pieces; there were even a few tears from people who couldn't pick everything up.

It's important to remember that the streets would be clean if just one person would pick up plastic in every neighbourhood. The song 'ABC' by The Jackson 5 inspired me to think of a motto that everyone should follow: One: See it. Two: Pick it up. Three: In the bin.

My work means I've now been named Youth Ambassador for Plastic Pollution Coalition and a Child Ambassador for HOW Global and World Cleanup Day. It makes me feel that I'm really doing something for the environment and that if my work keeps on growing, more and more people will know about plastic pollution and climate change.

Together, we can be a voice that will finally let humans and animals live in peace. If you want to campaign, follow your conscience and remember that you're campaigning not because you have to, but because it's the right thing to do.

Don't **BE DISCOURAGED** because **FUTURE GENERATIONS** are counting on **YOU.**

ZOE ROSENBERG, 16

HAPPY HEN ANIMAL SANCTUARY FOUNDER, ANIMAL RIGHTS ACTIVIST

Zoe Rosenberg grew up valuing the lives of all living things, including farm animals. When she saw the horrific reality of egg farms online, her family decided to rescue chickens that might have gone to the meat and food industry. They then transformed their backyard in to an animal sanctuary and began to save animal after animal.

But Zoe's backyard wasn't big enough for her plans. She wanted everyone to know how the food industry was treating animals, so she turned to protesting. She chained herself to slaughterhouses, livestreaming the entire thing on Facebook, and disrupted sports matches to get her message out there. And nothing could slow down her desire to show thousands of people how animals' basic rights were being stripped away to provide food for their tables.

Why do some people shrug off killing animals for food or fur, yet support locking others up for abusing the 'cuter' ones like cats and dogs? With time, Zoe hopes this question no longer needs to be asked and that all animals are treated with the same amount of respect.

ZOE

Over three thousand animals lose their lives every second at the hands of humans. I have seen hundreds of litres of blood being loaded into a garbage truck outside of a slaughterhouse; the blood of thousands of innocent lives spilling onto the streets. This sounds like a scene from a horror movie, but it was right here where I live in California.

I was raised with the understanding that animals are our friends, not our food. This feeling became stronger when my family decided to get chickens. When one of them called Popcorn fell ill, my mother and I spent hundreds of dollars on veterinary care. No one understood why we were willing to do so much for a chicken.

Shortly after Popcorn passed away, I came across a website that would change the course of my life forever. It was about an organisation in Australia, NSW Hen Rescue, that was rescuing chickens who would have been killed for meat. After watching one of its videos, I stopped eating eggs and stopped drinking cow's milk too, figuring that that was probably a similarly cruel industry. But my actions didn't feel like enough. Animals were still being treated this way and I wasn't doing anything to end it.

I emailed the Australian hen rescue's founder for advice on rescuing chickens in the US and asked my mum if we could do it. I spent over a month building the Happy Hen Animal Sanctuary website and rescued 12 hens. We eventually progressed to rescuing all farmed animals, and today have saved over 800 animals from factory farms, slaughterhouses, and other abusive situations.

It has been a beautiful yet tragic experience. Take chickens, for example. They have been genetically manipulated to lay over 300 eggs every year when they would only naturally lay eight to 12. This breeding method causes severe health issues.

This is really upsetting but I decided to turn this grief into action by organising and participating in protests. Some of the most impactful of these protests have been at Cal Poly University where I've been campaigning to shut down the university's slaughterhouse where animals are killed for meat.

I would like to eventually see animals be granted legal personhood. This doesn't mean the right to vote or run for office. The definition of personhood is "the quality or condition of being an individual person." Granting this would replace animals' current status as property and protect them from violence. It would mean that people couldn't legally eat them, experiment on them, use them for entertainment, or confine them in cages against their will. Activism can be scary but it's important to push yourself outside of your comfort zones because …

all successful movements throughout history have had to **PUSH THROUGH TOUGH TIMES**, and we will too!

ABBIE BARNES, 22
WILDLIFE CONSERVATION FILMMAKER

Do you appreciate the natural world? Or do you, like so many of us, take your surroundings for granted? Abbie Barnes doesn't want to shame people, but instead inspire them to #SpendMoreTimeInTheWILD. Through her filmmaking, she also teaches anyone who is willing to listen about the environmental issues facing the natural landscapes and why we need to preserve them.

Her first ever film was inspired by *Running Wild*, a Michael Morpurgo book. It introduced her to palm oil — a common supermarket ingredient derived from the fruits of the African oil palm tree. Huge forests are burned down in order to grow these trees and obtain the oil, which means the animals that live there such as orangutans, elephants and tigers are left without a home. Next came a look at the plight of the ocean in her film *Save Our Oceans*. That earned her the first-place award at the 2016 EcoTales Film Festival by the great David Attenborough. If that wasn't enough, she then climbed and filmed Mount Kilimanjaro!

Now, Abbie has moved her focus back home to the UK where she films some of the nation's best hiking spots. She also runs her own company, Song Thrush

Productions, where she uses film to passionately teach sustainability and inspire countless people to step outside their front door.

Her nature-loving audience is growing as each day goes by and, with it, a deeper recognition of the planet's beauty.

ABBIE

I've always felt at home in the natural world. When I was younger, I went to several different schools because I struggled so much with bullying. There was a point where I had to choose my identity: either conforming to the socially acceptable version of myself or actually just being myself, which meant being wild and covered in mud. I'm so glad I chose the second option.

Since then, I've been trying to pursue a more meaningful life. The more time you spend outside, the more you realise that the planet is being undermined by human activity in every possible way. I felt a burning passion to pursue environmental issues and make them approachable to the everyday person.

If we can get more people aspiring to create treasured memories in the natural world, then that will lead them to protect it. That's what I try to communicate with film. My first film was about the devastating effects of palm oil production on wildlife, especially orangutans. It won a competition when I was 15, allowing me to speak to politicians at the European Parliament about the importance of labelling ingredients. I then set up World Orangutan Day with a couple of people from around the world. Every year, we celebrate the orangutan and raise awareness of what we can all do to help them.

My next film focus was marine debris. We don't tend to care about the things we don't see but I had seen what washed up on the coast. So I made a video called *Save Our Oceans*, which involved arranging a beach clean, interviewing experts, and talking about how we could all help. That also won an award which I received from David Attenborough.

One of my most incredible experiences, however, was climbing Mount Kilimanjaro at the age of 18 to make a film about the effects of global climate change on glaciers and wildlife. It was my first time flying abroad solo, so I had a childlike sense of awe about everything. But I did struggle. I accidentally watered my camera (which killed it) and suffered from altitude sickness, but I had to keep going. Reaching the top was like reaching the summit of my life.

It's very hard to tell people what's going on with the environment without them feeling shame or being overwhelmed. I even find myself feeling insignificant when researching issues, but I have to rise above it. As well as being mentally demanding, a lot of the films I shoot now are also physically stressful. I recently walked 1,100 kilometres (700 miles) in two months, shooting from dawn until dusk, and at night too.

I do all of this because we need to wake up to the reality of these issues. Most people know what they should be doing to help, but it's about recognising our values, both as individuals and together as a group. Avoiding single-use items, buying environmentally sensitive products, and planning ahead to car share, walk, or cycle will make a difference. Governments also need to step up, for example by telling supermarkets to reduce excess plastic packaging and food waste. None of these changes have to be uncomfortable. In fact, you may find they give you a more meaningful life and improve your sense of self-worth.

Right now, I'm focusing on producing more online hiking adventures and group walking events that create a worldwide community of courageous people. It's utterly incredible that I get messages from individuals all around the world telling me how my work has inspired them. People who are struggling with their mental health and have been stuck inside for weeks have gone outside after watching my videos and those with disabilities who are unable to go outside are accessing the natural environment through them. It makes everything so worthwhile and goes to show that

with a little PLANNING, ANYONE CAN MAKE A DIFFERENCE.

The world needs more passionate people, so think about what makes you come alive and go after that.

Don't worry about tomorrow, focus on being the best you can be right now.

ABBIE BARNES

JAMIE MARGOLIN, 17

ZERO HOUR FOUNDER, CLIMATE CHANGE ACTIVIST

Jamie Margolin grew up watching political satire and news shows on TV with her dad. But it wasn't until recently that she decided to get in to politics herself and take a forceful stand against politicians who say they care about the environment yet do nothing to prove it.

In 2017, dry humid weather caused wildfires in Canada, covering Jamie's home in Seattle in a dirty grey smog. News channels failed to link it to climate change, so Jamie turned to social media, organising youths across the country to march for the world they deserved.

Her movement is called Zero Hour because the time to act is now. The number of environmental disasters is going up and our access to clean air and chemical-free food is becoming more and more scarce. As Jamie and her fellow youth campaigners point out, we are no longer dealing with ifs and buts; we are now dealing with when.

Jamie's organisation is going straight to young people, educating reams of school students and organising a huge week of action, plus a must-attend concert in Miami. She's hoping to reignite the climate change conversation and, at the same time, force the US government to change its attitude. It's an extremely difficult task, but not an impossible one.

JAMIE

CLIMATE JUSTICE is not about saving something separate from ourselves, but about **SAVING OURSELVES**.

Fossil fuels are what power most of our modern society, but they're coming at a huge cost. For hundreds of years, we've been emitting huge amounts of pollution and greenhouse gases into the air.

I believe the reason this climate crisis hasn't been stopped yet is because of corporate greed. Governments and companies would rather make money than stop and save humanity. We shouldn't be naming hurricanes things like Maria and Katrina. We should be naming them after companies like ExxonMobil and Shell Oil.

In 2017, I noticed that few people were drawing the connection between all of these natural disasters or pointing out the fact that they were arguably all man-made. I also became frustrated that leaders who didn't represent my generation were deciding our future. I was under voting age (and still am now) so was feeling powerless.

So that summer, I sent out a call on social media for a youth climate march. A few people liked the idea, but I was waiting for someone else to take charge. I soon realised that if I didn't do it, nothing was going to happen. I've always been an organiser within my local community but had never organised something on this scale before. We were a group of kids with no funding and people didn't believe in us. But for several months, we brainstormed, eventually releasing the Zero Hour website and an official plan of action.

We decided to hold the march in Washington DC. A bunch of us stayed in one tiny house for two weeks and more people started to support us. Media visited us and actors from Black Panther and other Marvel movies publicly encouraged us. On the day of the march, it didn't just rain. It poured. I received flood alert warnings on my phone and thought no one would turn up. But a thousand people still came. Most were young and first-time protesters. We took to the streets and danced in the rain; it was such a beautiful event.

I've also been working to get politicians on board. At the moment, they get a gold star for just saying they believe in climate change. Our governor in Washington state is praised for being a "green" governor, but a huge natural gas terminal is still being built that will affect the lives of the indigenous people living near it and the air pollution levels of the state as a whole. The first step to getting out of a hole is to stop digging, yet the state is still giving permits to polluters and still endangering our future.

This encouraged me to sue the state, not alone but with a non-profit organisation called Our Children's Trust. In the US, we have the constitutional right to life, liberty, and the pursuit of happiness. But you can't have any of those things without clean air and water.

At first, we tried to work with the government. When that didn't work, we ended up suing them and the court ruled in our favour. Although we've had a bunch of victories like this, they haven't resulted in real change. It's escalated to the point where we're now in the process of suing the government for our rights; rights which the government has denied.

People always ask, "What's next? What's going to top the march?" You see other movements around you churning out campaign after campaign and receiving huge amounts of funding, and you feel pressured to catch up. But you're tired, you're human, and you have school. I'm still trying to figure out how to balance everything, but have come up with Zero Hour's next campaign which will see us spending the school year educating students then holding a giant week of action in Miami in the summer.

Although we focus on national campaigns, the real work happens at the local level, so get together with your community and figure out the issues that are damaging your environment and lives. Systems are trying to divide and conquer, to make us individualistic and not think in a community sense, so we have to combat that with organisation. People need something to fight for rather than just to fight against, and nothing beats the power of movement.

KEHKASHAN BASU, 18
ENVIRONMENTALIST, GREEN HOPE FOUNDATION FOUNDER

In just six years, Kehkashan Basu and her team in Dubai have planted more than 15 thousand trees, cleaned over 100 beaches, and recycled more than 100 tonnes of waste. Her environmental organisation Green Hope Foundation has hundreds of members. They come from all over the world but have united to achieve one goal: a sustainable Earth.

Green Hope started small – just Kehkashan and a few friends from her school in Dubai. But it grew and grew, planting its roots in to country after country. Kehkashan doesn't speak the language of every person she meets, but through song, drama, and sport she teaches thousands of young people the truth about the environment. In doing so she creates lasting memories that help transform children who haven't had the opportunity to access education into passionate eco-warriors.

Kehkashan has become the voice of future generations. She has spoken at several United Nations forums and, in 2016, was awarded the International Children's Peace Prize. Her ultimate goal is for Green Hope to have a presence in all 193 countries of the world. Some may say that uniting the entire planet is impossible, but

Kehkashan is hellbent on achieving it.

KEHKASHAN

I once attended a lecture by the famous environmentalist Robert Swan. He said: "The greatest threat to our planet is the belief that someone else will save it." Those words made me realise that society's indifference and lack of awareness were the main reasons for our current state of affairs.

We have taken our environment for granted. We produce enormous amounts of waste, we hunt species to extinction, and, to top it all, we burn fossil fuels which send billions of tonnes of carbon dioxide into the atmosphere contributing to global warming. Earth's temperature has been rising dangerously and, as a result, we are witnessing violent storms, forest fires, melting polar ice caps, and rising sea levels; all of which are threatening life on our planet.

I was born on World Environment Day; my parents told me it was fate that I would become an environmental crusader. When I was very young, I saw an image of a dead bird with a stomach full of plastic. My parents explained the impact of plastic pollution and I was so shocked that I went around my neighbourhood asking shopkeepers and residents to stop using plastic and to properly dispose of their waste. People were very supportive.

On my eighth birthday, I used my gift money to plant my first tree. My efforts caught the attention of the local media and I was invited to speak at an Indonesian conference organised

by the United Nations Environment Programme (UNEP). This was my first step into the international arena.

I was then invited to the 2012 Earth Summit in Brazil. Over 50 thousand delegates were there — heads of state, policymakers, civil society leaders — but only a handful of children. Our future was being debated by adults who would not be around to live through it. I thought this was extremely unfair so I established Green Hope to provide a platform for the youth to take local and global actions to promote sustainability.

In 2012, I was elected as the Global Coordinator for UNEP's Major Groups for Children and Youth, making me the youngest person in the world to ever hold the position. Adults were initially very doubting and didn't take me seriously. But I've never allowed that to deter me. I've always told them: "Look at my work, not at my age."

What began as a 12-year-old's dream is now a global social innovation movement with over a thousand youth members across the world. Our mission is to use sustainable development education as a tool to empower children, especially those who are marginalised.

I use music, drama, art, and sport to teach young people and, through these Environment Academies, have educated over seven thousand children in more than 20 countries. These include hundreds of Syrian refugees, orphans, and HIV+ children in Nepal, poor and homeless children across India, and children from indigenous Amazonian tribes.

There are more than two billion youths in the world today.

Every one of us has the potential
to be a **CHANGEMAKER** and define
our own **DESTINY**.

If you are focused and persistent, you can achieve your
dreams. My, and Green Hope's, journey is a testament to that.

LOOK AT MY WORK, NOT MY AGE.

KEHKASHAN BASU

JASILYN CHARGER, 22

WATER PROTECTOR

The experiences of Native American people are rarely heard, but 22-year-old Jasilyn Charger has been battling for her community to have a voice.

When oil companies were given the go ahead to build pipelines under the rivers near her home, she took on the US government to stop the contamination of her people's water.

When Native American young people weren't even being listened to by their own leaders, she founded a youth council so they could have their say. And to take a stand, she has done everything from running 2,000-kilometres to deliver a petition, to peacefully protesting when law enforcement descended on her protest campsite.

Everything Jasilyn does is to help her community. Not only does she try to protest for environmental causes, but she works to improve the mental health crisis that has ravaged the North American youth.

She hasn't won every fight; the Dakota Access Pipeline that she desperately tried to stop was signed off by President Donald Trump and is currently pumping oil underneath the Missouri river. Her people were thrown in prison for standing up for their rights. Her hard work was torn down in front of her very eyes. Despite all of that, she still has the courage and determination to accept another battle. Because, eventually, she knows that she will win.

JASILYN

Living on the Cheyenne River Eagle Butte reservation was a fight for survival. I grew up in a mental health facility and was homeless for six months after I turned 18. I didn't have anyone to go to and got in to drugs and alcohol. A really nice family then helped me get on my feet and get sober.

I eventually came back to Cheyenne River for my friend's funeral. There was just funeral after funeral after funeral. Young people were killing themselves and it got so severe that we young people took it upon ourselves to step up and create the One Mind Youth Movement. We have been fighting for a safe house for our youth to go to that is run by us and not the government. It will give young people a place to stay for the night and a person to talk to if they need it.

We have also been fighting an even tougher battle. Water is so important in our culture because it was our first medicine. Our people have used it as part of the healing process throughout history. So, when oil pipelines that would be dug extremely close to our water supply were announced, I, and other young people, knew we had to fight. We defeated one pipeline in 2015 (although it was later approved by the new government) and heard a radio announcement asking for people to come to a meeting about the Dakota Access Pipeline. The adults that organised the meet-up were really surprised to see a bunch of young kids trying to help.

In order to halt the pipeline, everyone decided to make a camp at the Standing Rock Sioux reservation. In the beginning, there were only five of us, but that number slowly grew. A lot of men in our community didn't believe in us at first. They said we weren't going to make a difference because no one would listen. We said: "It's fine if you don't want to fight for yourselves, but we're going to fight for you."

It was initially hard to get the chairmen from different tribes to cooperate. But we wanted to show that if the youth from different tribes could organise themselves, our leaders could work together and come up with a plan to stop the pipeline. So, the youth from lots of tribes ran to Washington DC together to deliver a petition signed by over 100 thousand people. Seeing us campaigning as one group encouraged our leaders to start communicating too.

When the hostility rose between the police and the Native Americans in the camp, our men became very angry. They went to the frontline where the police were based, but we stood in front of them and stopped them from retaliating with violence. We still all experienced the police firing rubber bullets, spraying us with mace and hosing us down with cold water. But we wanted to stand together in a peaceful protest and so we didn't strike back.

Unfortunately, the plans still went ahead and right now, the Dakota Access Pipeline is laid in the ground and there's oil going through it. But I'm fighting another pipeline on my reservation. It's 28 kilometres from my family and 13 kilometres from the nearest community. These communities are really rural. There's no police stations, grocery stores or hospitals. A lot of the youth trek from community to community or go horseback riding, and they won't be able to do that if the pipeline is built. But we're more prepared this time, and are going to approach this in a very organised way.

Sometimes I wish I could just stay home and be normal. But this is the road I ended up walking. Not every Native American gets this chance so I take advantage of the fact that I can tell our story and where we come from.

No matter how **SCARY** or **UNFAIR** life can be, know that **YOU CAN MAKE A CHANGE**.

If you have the strength and courage to create that ripple, it will expand. You are not alone; we youths will support and encourage you. We may not be in the same place but we are connected.

MIKAILA ULMER, 14

ME & THE BEES LEMONADE FOUNDER,
CONSERVATIONIST, ENTREPRENEUR

Mikaila Ulmer has always been an entrepreneur. When she was really young, she dreamt up ideas for companies that would help her make enough money to buy toys. But an encounter with a bee changed everything. Mikaila's parents taught her how important the buzzy insects are to the environment and she started thinking about how her profits could go toward helping them instead ...

"What could I sell?" Mikaila thought to herself. The answer turned out to be lemonade. Mikaila used her great grandmother's flaxseed lemonade recipe and added a smidge of honey made by bees. She called the modern recipe Me & The Bees Lemonade. Since 2009, she has been producing and selling this lemonade and donating a portion of the profits to bee-saving organisations. She is one of the youngest CEOs in the US and has managed to get her bottles stocked in over 650 stores across the country.

Mikaila's efforts have been publicly praised by former President Barack Obama and earned her various young entrepreneur awards. Now, she has started her own non-profit organisation aimed at keeping even more bees safe and healthy. She does it all with the help of her family.

Knowing that other children may never have this support spurs her on to become even more successful too, so that she has the money to invest in other young people's world-changing ideas.

Buy a bottle and save a bee. It really is that simple.

MIKAILA

When I was four, I signed up to a kids' entrepreneurship contest. To enter, I needed a product. Just as I was trying to think of an idea, I received a cookbook from my great granny Helen. It was from the 1940s and contained her flaxseed lemonade recipe. Around the same time, I was also stung by two bees in one week. I was pretty terrified, but my parents didn't want me to be afraid of bees, so they told me to do some research.

After watching some videos and reading some books, I learned that bees are super important to our ecosystem and to our food chain. They are believed to pollinate one out of every three bites of food we eat, even completely unordinary things like pizza. Here's how. Bees pollinate alfalfa, which is then eaten by cows. Cows make dairy which is turned into cheese. That cheese then goes on your pizza.

When I learned that bees were dying at an alarming rate, I decided to mix my great granny's recipe with honey and then donate a portion of the proceeds to organisations that were helping save the bees. Me & The Bees Lemonade has definitely grown a lot more than I imagined it would when I was four years old.

I started it at a lemonade stand and eventually, a Whole Foods Market near to my house asked to stock it. Now it's in over 650 stores across the US, from New York to California. I also recently started a non-profit organisation called The Healthy Hive Foundation to educate people about why bees are important and carry out important research that may protect bees.

It can be pretty hard being a student, a 14-year-old girl, and the owner of a company, and still have a regular life. I often have to travel for work and do homework at the same time. But it's worth it. A lot of people tell me that I've inspired them to take a stand and do something they were afraid of. I hope that continues to happen and that more young entrepreneurs go for their dreams. I want to see parents being more supportive of these ambitions too.

I'd also like to see a change in the business world. More companies should have a cause or charity they support. In the future, I want to be able to invest in other companies run by minorities such as women, African Americans, and the youth.

Being an ENTREPRENEUR isn't just about having ONE GOOD IDEA but being CREATIVE and finding business IDEAS in EVERYDAY LIFE.

There's always a way to monetise an issue and use that money to help solve it. It doesn't have to be a really big issue; helping a smaller cause is just as worthwhile.

And if you want to help the bees, join my mission, or my hive as I like to call it. One of the biggest problems I have is needing more people to purchase my lemonade to let store owners know that there's a demand for it. So, if there isn't a store that stocks my lemonade near you, ask one if they can carry Me & The Bees, and, hopefully, they'll send over an order!

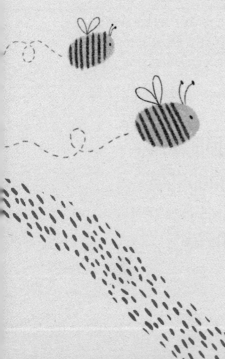

POLITICS and SOCIAL JUSTICE

Should we be able to go about our daily lives without a constant feeling of dread? Should we feel empowered to speak out against our governments without fear of persecution? And should everyone have a right to freedom and happiness, no matter where they are born? Most people would answer yes to all of these questions. Yet in many places, a world like that does not exist.

But now, young people are taking a stand. People of different races and religions are opening up about the different abuses they face. From being discriminated against because of the colour of their skin, to the hostility refugees commonly experience after fleeing their war-torn countries; campaigners are pointing out the facts that lots of people don't want to hear. And in doing so, they are raising awareness, calling for change, and putting pressure on authorities such as the government and the police to make the world a safer and better place. Most of all, they are being heard.

You see, myself and the following Resisters I'm going to introduce you to don't think it's too much to ask that people wake up each morning without wondering which kind of harassment they're going to face. That children can go to school without fear. And that people can go home each evening to a home, not a makeshift tent in the middle of a camp but a real house with a roof, lighting and electricity.

It's not too much to ask because we are all the same. No matter where we are born or what our identity is, we have the same genetic make up. We feel the same things, we share the same dreams. We are not more entitled to something than another. We all deserve a place to belong.

The young women featured on the following pages are working to achieve this by opening people's eyes to the injustices that many have ignored for too long. Together, they will make the world a fairer place. All they need is your support.

ASHA AND IMA CHRISTIAN, 20 AND 21

APP DEVELOPERS AND TECHNOLOGY EDUCATORS

In 2014, Asha and Ima Christian, together with their brother Caleb, launched an app called Five-O. It dealt with a topic that makes law enforcement in America very uncomfortable: police brutality.

Did you know that the police killed around a thousand people in the US in 2017 alone and near a quarter of the dead were black citizens? Racial profiling has long existed in several parts of the world, but it is America that has some of the most shocking statistics surrounding this. In the US, African American people are statistically more likely to be stopped and searched by police, are often treated violently even when arrested for a non-violent crime, and have been killed by law enforcement despite being unarmed.

Asha and Ima saw how black children, teenagers, and adults were being unfairly targeted. They were particularly saddened by the death of unarmed 18-year-old, Michael Brown, who was fatally shot by a white police officer in 2014. His killing ignited several protests and an investigation in to the racial bias of the police force and court system in Ferguson, Missouri. The US Department of Justice found that there was indeed a pattern of racial bias in Ferguson's police department and court system, but the police officer responsible for Brown's death was exonerated of any criminal wrongdoing.

Yet the siblings knew there had to be a way to stop police from committing violent – or even unlawful – acts. So, they designed an app. Five-O allows people to document incidents and interactions they've had with the police – both good and bad – and lets citizens rate their county police department. It also gives police the opportunity to organise events and form a more positive relationship with communities. This has been hugely successfully across a few major cities.

By seeing exactly how technology could be used for good, Asha and Ima are now passing their knowledge onto other young people in the US, but also in Guyana, a country in South America, by running tech-focused classes. With the sisters' help, young people are learning all the great things technology can do and are being given the skills to create solutions to their country's problems. An app here and a website there may be all it takes to transform negativity and tragedy into hope and peace.

ASHA & IMA

Our parents have always taken the time to make sure we believed we could do anything. Our mum was actually the person who first introduced us to technology. She bought us a LEGO Mindstorms Robotics kit and we couldn't put it down. When we were in middle school, we had to take a technology class. There, we were introduced to basic app development and coding. (We did project-based learning which is much more exciting and satisfying. We'd recommend that to any young person wanting to learn how to code.)

We had been paying attention to the scary things happening in the world. We talked to our parents about issues, such as the Michael Brown case, and they put everything in to context. They stressed that we should focus on finding solutions, so we decided to create an app. We threw all of our ideas onto a whiteboard and developed Five-O in around six months.

People who work in law enforcement, such as police officers are no better or worse than the average citizen, but they are powerful and what they choose to do with that power is what counts. We wanted our app to give every citizen a voice. We wanted there to be a balance so people could document both positive and negative interactions with the police. Law enforcement agencies with positive reviews could then act as role models for those with negative ones.

Five-O was a potential solution to a very emotional and serious problem for many people. We received a lot of attention in the media and got over ten thousand downloads within the first few weeks. It was a real success in cities such as Houston and New York where we were able to compile enough data to combine ratings and produce an accurate grade for their policing districts.

In this process, we realised we had other app and project ideas too, so we created Pinetart Inc to house them. The company has done so much, from creating Community Tech Days for students in our local area to developing STEMGuyana; an organisation that runs robotics camps throughout Guyana. Our entire family is Guyanese, so choosing that particular place was a no-brainer. We have taught hundreds of students there and continue to reach more with each programme.

We are firm believers that the best way to solve problems in disadvantaged communities is to put technology into the hands of those who are directly affected. We hope to create a foundation that will financially support young people who have those amazing and innovative ideas. We have to champion individual thought because our current education system doesn't create innovators, doers, or thinkers.

MUZOON ALMELLEHAN, 20
EDUCATION ACTIVIST AND UNICEF GOODWILL AMBASSADOR

Born in the Syrian city of Daraa, Muzoon Almellehan's early childhood was spent being a regular kid. She enjoyed going to school and spending time with her family and friends. And she dreamed of becoming a journalist, reporting on the suffering people across the world face. But then came her own experience of suffering: war and conflict.

Muzoon and her family bravely fled their home in 2013, spending almost three years living in refugee camps in Jordan. She was determined to continue learning so she went to the camps' schools, but was surprised to see that half of the girls in her class dropped out during the school year.

She knew her classmates were losing the best chance of a future they may ever have, so she pleaded with the girls' parents and she taught them what education could provide for the girls. Then the international children's organisation UNICEF heard of Muzoon's campaign and helped her too, eventually naming her its youngest ever Goodwill Ambassador at the time.

In late 2015, Muzoon arrived in Newcastle in the UK, still hoping to get a full education. She did just that, enrolling in school and later earning a place at university. Today, she balances her studies with travelling the world to meet other refugee children learning in schools supported by UNICEF, and campaigns for the millions still struggling to get an education.

One day, Muzoon hopes to return to, and help rebuild, Syria so that world leaders can see how education can create a better future for all. War has the ability to tear countries apart but, with Muzoon's help, it will hopefully no longer have the power to rip children's lives in two.

MUZOON

My father taught me that knowledge, once you have it, is the one thing that no one can take away from you. Before the fighting in Syria erupted, my life was one of hope, safety, and warmth. But we Syrians dreamed of freedom, the freedom that Syria hasn't yet secured.

In 2011, the revolution broke out and, soon after, the conflict began. For the next two years, my family and I lived under siege. My father wasn't able to go to work anymore and I couldn't see my friends as much as I used to. My beloved country became unrecognisable and my journey to school became too dangerous, as did sitting in the classroom I once felt safe in.

When the shelling became more intense, my dad finally made the difficult choice to flee our home. He told me I could only pack a bag, so I collected a book of memories and letters that my friends had made for me and my school books. I was scared I would never be able to return to school.

It took until early morning to reach a place close to the border. We had to wait until dark before we could go to the border itself. We travelled on buses and then walked for three hours to Zaatari refugee camp. Once there, we were given a small tent; there was no electricity and it was bitterly cold but I was relieved to find there was a school. It was only once I entered I realised there weren't many children inside the classroom at all. I asked some girls in my class why this was. They said families had lost hope and thought the best option for their daughters was to find a man for them to marry. It was at this moment that I started my campaign.

I went from tent to tent, telling families what my father had told me: that education would open more doors for their daughters than early marriage ever could. Some people chose to argue, but others changed their mindset. One day, I heard that people had started calling me the Malala of Syria. When she visited the camp, I got the chance to meet her. We shared our souls and our goals, and became great friends.

After nearly three years, my family and I were told we were being resettled in Newcastle in the UK. I was excited about having a warm home and a space to study. I had taught myself English and now I was going to get a chance to use it every day. It was very hard to get used to a new culture and an English accent that I hadn't heard before. But day by day, everything became easier.

I'm **PROUD** to be a **WOMAN**,
I'm proud to be **SYRIAN**,
and I'm proud to be a **REFUGEE**.

I'm never going to stop until my mission is complete and will never forget the people who are still living in the camps and all the people suffering back in Syria. In 2017, I travelled to Chad with UNICEF to meet children whose education had been disrupted by the Boko Haram crisis. The stories from the young people I met will stay with me forever, as will the glimmer of hope in each of their voices.

The only way to make use of these young people's potential is through education. Think how their knowledge could transform our world into a more equal, fair, and peaceful place for us all to live. We cannot risk giving up the fight for education because, in the middle of the darkness, learning gives you light.

IN thE miDDLe OF THE dARKnESS, LEaRNiNg Gives yOU LiGHT.

MUZOON ALMELLEHAN

LANE MURDOCK, 16

GUN CONTROL ACTIVIST,
NATIONAL SCHOOL WALKOUT FOUNDER

In 2012, a 20-year-old man killed 20 children and six adults at Sandy Hook Elementary School in Connecticut, US. Lane Murdock remembers this because the mass shooting, which was just a 20-minute drive from her house, was so close to home and was the first time she'd ever seen her mother so visibly upset.

Gun control still divides a lot of America. The Second Amendment of the United States Constitution was drawn up in the 18th century and is one of the supreme laws of the US. It states that American people have the right to keep and bear arms. This means that many people believe they have the right to own firearms for things such as self-defence, hunting, and sport. But a rise in mass shootings has sparked debate over whether this law is outdated, who should be allowed to buy weapons, and what kind of weapons the average person should be able to buy. States in the US have varying gun restriction laws and it is the loopholes in these laws that have often allowed people with troubled pasts to purchase extremely powerful guns, resulting in multiple deaths.

Lane watched shooting after shooting unfold on the news, particularly those targeted at schools, and felt a responsibility to do something. Then in 2018, a teenage boy killed 14 students and three staff members at Marjory Stoneman Douglas (MSD) High School in Florida. Lane felt like she had to act. She organised a walkout at her school to protest these horrific acts of gun violence and call the government to change gun laws. But little did Lane know that her powerful words would result in hundreds of thousands of students across America walking out too!

Phase two of Lane's strategy is called WalkoutToVote. This encourages every student old enough to go out and vote at every election, because the only way to make the change you desire is to create it yourself by voting, speaking out, and doing everything you can to raise awareness.

And that's exactly what Lane is planning to do.

LANE

I've always made sure to speak up if I felt something was wrong. But, like most kids, I never really thought about the rest of the world, until I saw the pain in my own mother after she heard about Sandy Hook. Parents try to be strong for their children, but that event had a major impact on me.

When I first heard about the shooting at MSD in Florida, I wasn't shocked. I just felt numb. I was angry and freaked out by how indifferent teenagers had become to school shootings. So, I went home, went on the petition website Change.org, and proposed the National School Walkout.

A walkout seemed perfect because it put the power in students' hands and was peaceful, not violent. I didn't tell people how to do it, I just recommended what to do. March For Our Lives, a movement set up by MSD survivors, hadn't emerged yet so I was nervous that there wouldn't be a youth movement, but I'm happy to have been proven wrong.

On the day of the walkout, we had at the very least ten walkouts in every state in America. It was weird that an idea in my head had turned into a national protest. It felt a bit like a wedding. You plan and plan, but the day goes by so quickly and you feel like you were never there! People were telling me that Barack Obama had said this, and some other important person had said that, but I was so busy that I felt like I missed it.

I definitely felt burned out during the process. Some of my friends took command and I've recently started to dip my toe back in. Social media became addictive too. It's where the youth movement is right now, but when you go online it's hard to get past the idea that you're constantly missing out on something. If you're a regular teenage girl, you often think you're missing an event that your friends went to, for example. And if you're a teenage activist, you think you've missed an important protest or speech. Missing a Twitter thread almost has a deep political weight. But when you step back, you realise you're really not missing anything at all!

Before you get into activism, you must be aware of who you are. It's easy to lose yourself in the thoughts of the young activist group, so it's important to know what makes you different.

I'm an **ACTIVIST** but I'm also Lane Murdock.
Some days, **DANCING AROUND** and doing
DAVID BOWIE IMPRESSIONS are very
important to me and I don't care how many
people walked out.

I went from someone who is creative, bookish, loved going out, and being sociable to being someone who was doing interviews and shaking hands. Finding the crossing between the two is going to be my personal goal, but we have to realise we're not going to change gun laws alone. We can educate ourselves, but it's not a 16-year-old's responsibility to understand everything about political science. Adults got us in to this mess and it's up to them to help us get out of it.

My main message has always been:

If you're making someone **UNCOMFORTABLE**,
you're probably doing something **RIGHT**.

As a young activist, you're going to want to please as many people as possible, but that's not how you get change done. You need to make some noise. You need to be loud.

MAYA GHAZAL, 19

SPOKESPERSON FOR REFUGEE RIGHTS

Maya Ghazal didn't have to face the treacherous – and sometimes fatal – journey from Syria to Europe. But her father did. In 2014, he left his war-torn home to find a better life in the UK. Fifteen months later, he secured a visa for Maya and her family who then safely travelled to join him.

When she arrived in Birmingham, Maya was full of hope and ambition, but was surprised to find that refugees weren't exactly welcome. She found it hard to make friends and was rejected by numerous schools.

She was still learning the English language when a charity called The Children's Society asked her to give a speech about her religion. The organisation was so impressed that they offered her more chances to speak in front of an audience. Her inspiring talks detail the challenges of being a refugee and advise people how they can help. She even met Princes William and Harry when they gave her the Diana Award in 2017!

Maya's determination to get the future she deserved scored her a place at university studying aviation engineering. She dreams of becoming a pilot, but will also never stop working to change people's lives for the better.

MAYA

In Syria, I was just a typical teenager with a big family and a big group of friends. I wanted to study political science, visit the US, and eventually work in an embassy to represent my country. I also dreamed of seeing Big Ben and attending a One Direction concert — I used to be a big fan.

I'm not sure how my dad ended up in the UK; we don't really speak about his journey. But it was pretty straightforward for my mother, younger brothers and me, as my dad had applied for a family visa. However, it did take two attempts and 15 months of waiting until we were reunited with him in Birmingham.

When I came to the UK, I had high expectations. I thought we would carry on our lives like nothing had changed, but I was wrong. I wanted to go to school. I know school isn't a typical 16-year-old's favourite place, but I cared about my education and future.

I applied to schools by myself and was turned away from several for no good reason. It's true that my English wasn't the best. It was a new language for me and I was dealing with the Birmingham accent as well! I already had my Syrian GCSEs but wanted to further my education and sit in a classroom interacting with other students. Eventually, a college agreed to give me a place.

A month after I arrived in the UK, I was asked to say a few words about my religion at an event held by The Children's Society. I didn't know what to say or how to say it. Speaking English wasn't my strongest skill, nor writing speeches. But I practised that speech for three weeks and felt so good when I said it.

A staff member asked me to help other young people like me. I accepted because I knew it wasn't fair for any child to feel isolated, lonely, and rejected from education. I didn't know how far I could go back then.

All I wanted was to **SUPPORT OTHERS** and show that the smallest act of **KINDNESS** can **CHANGE** someone's life.

I started off speaking in Sunday church services, eventually spreading my message online and on TV channels and radio stations. A year later, I spoke in Parliament about the importance of education and tackling issues refugees face when they arrive in a new country.

Refugees didn't choose this life. We had homes, cars and an education. We don't want to be a burden to other countries; we want to live normal lives. But we can't control what happened. Sometimes, the best solution is to leave everything you built for the safety of your family.

At first, I didn't like the word "refugee". I didn't want to be seen as a person who was uneducated or sad or broken. But now, the word represents strength and resilience to me. Refugees unwillingly lost everything they built, yet are still succeeding, keeping a smile on their faces and hope in their hearts.

If I end up as a pilot, I want to prove that everything is possible as long as you believe in yourself. I know I might face discrimination from those who stereotype Arab people as being a threat. Hopefully, after I put in the work, the respected person flying an aeroplane will be the same person who was once underestimated and seen as a burden.

I am just at the beginning of my journey and I will do whatever I can to inspire others along the way.

NOA GUR GOLAN, 20
PACIFIST AND CONSCIENTIOUS OBJECTOR

When children living in Israel reach the age of 18, they have to join the army. Women must carry out this military service for a minimum of two years; men just under three. Noa Gur Golan didn't plan to break these rules until she was awarded a scholarship to an international school. It was there that she first heard the other side of the Israeli-Palestinian conflict that has been ongoing since 1948, and there that she realised how normal violence and hatred had become to young Israelis.

When she returned home, she joined the Women Wage Peace (WWP) movement — a campaign calling for a non-violent agreement to be drawn up and signed by both Israel and Palestine — and told her family she wouldn't be joining the army because she believed in peace. Not only is refusing military service rare in Israel but doing so on the grounds of pacifism is even rarer. Noa stuck to her belief and did it anyway. But her request was denied, and she was even sent to prison for her actions.

Yet she didn't lose faith. She educated the other prisoners about her anti-war message and continued to speak out when she was released for the final time. Although the other members of WWP have a peaceful mindset, they don't agree with Noa's refusal to take part in military service, preferring to use tactics such as marches instead. But Noa is glad that she drew attention to herself. She knows there is a more peaceful way to resolve things than conflict. And she won't stop battling to make that happen, even if everyone else urges her to back down.

NOA

The army is a huge part of life in Israel. It's seen as a way of giving back to your country. It was obvious that I would sign up until I experienced the Gaza War and realised that I didn't know much about the conflict or even about my own opinions.

When I went to school in Italy, it was the first time I had met Palestinians and Muslims. I spent two years there, building and shaping my identity. But it was still hard for me to accept that I wasn't going into the army.

My original dream was to be a combative pilot, but then I thought I could do something educational in the military instead. I soon realised the system wouldn't accept my values of peace and that any role I played in the army would mean taking part in a military system that I didn't agree with. My mum was really mad with my decision, so were my brothers. They asked me why I thought I was better than them and everyone else.

At first, I didn't want to refuse publicly. I just wanted an exemption so I could do civic service, which involves

volunteering in sectors such as education, instead. There are three ways to get an exemption from military service. For women, you either have to say that you are religious, that you have a physical or mental issue, or that you are a pacifist.

I wrote a letter explaining my beliefs and was invited to stand in front of a committee of military men. For an hour, they attacked me with questions that weren't even related to pacifism. After months of waiting, I was told that they had rejected my request because they didn't believe I was a pacifist. I tried again, and they rejected it again. I then had two options: either to lie or to refuse. I chose to refuse. And when you refuse, you go to prison.

I was sentenced four times; each time for between 20 to 30 days. I spent around four months in total in a military prison where army life was everything. I still had a uniform, I still had commanders, and I still had to do military work. I found it very uncomfortable. What happened to me wasn't fair, but I feel very complete with what I did. When something is unjust, sometimes it's necessary to take a stand.

So many movements try to bring change but sometimes they don't know how to communicate their ideas. I want to help them.

The main route to a **BETTER FUTURE**
is learning how to be with more **EMPATHY**.
This will lead to people understanding that
everyone has the **RIGHT TO LIVE FREE**,
the right to have their own country,
and the right to build their own **IDENTITY**.

I don't know what the exact solution is for Israel but I hope there will be two independent nations that will have freedom of movement. That's the most important thing to me.

BANA ALABED, 9

CAMPAIGNING FOR PEACE AND CHILDREN'S EDUCATION

Bana Alabed has experienced a great many things that no child should. Her house was bombed while she was playing inside; she lost her best friend; and she had to stop going to school while the civil war that has been devastating her country for the last eight years raged on.

Bana grew up in the Syrian city of Aleppo; one of the main battlefields of the country's ongoing civil war. In late 2016, she began tweeting about the daily lives of children who were growing up in the middle of all the fighting. Her mother Fatemah helped her. An early tweet read: "My name is Bana, I'm 7 years old. I am talking to the world now live from East Aleppo. This is my last moment to either live or die."

She used social media in a truly powerful way, calling out to world leaders for peace on Twitter and reminding her 300-thousand followers about the war's human cost. Thankfully, Bana and her family were evacuated to Turkey. There, she wrote her powerful book, *Dear World*, describing how her childhood was ripped apart by war.

Bana continues to use her platform to fight for the rights of children whose voices have been taken away, and has had the courage to stand up for global peace in rooms full of political and business leaders. At just nine years old, Bana's voice is already strong. As she gets older, it's only set to become even more powerful.

BANA

Life in Syria before the war was like every other place in this world. We could do anything we wanted. I had a lovely childhood and loved being around babies, so I asked my mother if we could have one. A few months later, she told me I would get my wish.

But after both my brothers were born, things started changing. People were kidnapped and bombs would go off. My mother and father became scared, so when I was around the age of three, we moved to a different home so we would feel safer. Adults became my friends; I liked to listen to their conversations. My father's friends then started bringing their children round to our house, so I could spend time and play with them. I still remember my two best friends. One stayed at my house with me for a long time; I don't know what happened to her after I left Syria.

When I started kindergarten, I was the cleverest girl there as my mother had already taught me the alphabet and all of the numbers. One day, I woke up to prepare myself for school and heard a loud noise. Glass fell down onto my bed and, in that moment, everything changed.

I lost a lot of things to the bombs. I lost touch with almost all of my family: my grandma, my grandpa, my uncles. I lost my other best friend and my school. I had to spend my life at home. There was no going outside, no learning, no having fun. The world didn't know what was really happening. Our hospital was bombed; there weren't enough doctors and there wasn't enough clean water and food. We were dying from fear and hunger.

I decided I wanted to help all those children who DIDN'T HAVE A VOICE.

When I started tweeting, I hoped something would change. I didn't imagine that everyone would start listening and want to stop this war. When I read people's messages, it made me feel stronger. After a while, we heard that we would be leaving our home. I loved my home, but leaving was the best thing to save our lives. I still had hope that everything would change so I prayed that we could stay.

Then a bomb hit my house. I couldn't see anything; I could only hear voices. Someone carried me out and I started crying, not because I feared death or because my house was destroyed, but because I didn't know where my father or brother were. When we all eventually travelled to Turkey, it was heaven. The best thing about it was that it snowed in the winter. We were so happy and wanted to stay outside all the time.

I've done a lot of things to turn the world's attention to what is happening in Syria. I decided to write a book because I wanted everyone to know how I struggled and how I could only know happy moments when the warplanes stopped. I now talk about my experiences in front of a lot of people who are bigger than me. They listen and believe in me. They have given me a lot of strength to continue.

I do hope that I can go back to Syria one day. I would like to be a teacher and build schools for those children who haven't had an education. Or I'd love to be a doctor to remove pain from those children too. I want there to be no more wars in the world so every child can have the chance to do anything they want. A lot of children dream of being doctors, actors, or artists. So please give them a chance to live like normal children. I want to be like my mother. She gave me inspiration and taught me that the world is something that we can change if we want a better life for everyone.

KATIE SONES, 22

FOUNDER OF SOCIALLY CONSCIOUS BEAUTY BRAND LIPSLUT

If you ask someone to donate money to a cause, they will often shake their head and run away as fast as they can. People percieve that they have little money to give away, but they don't mind splurging on luxuries such as make-up. Katie Sones noticed this precisely at the time of President Donald Trump's inauguration – and her socially concious beauty brand, Lipslut, was born.

While studying for a university degree in the US, Katie sourced a high-quality formula and reliable manufacturers, and got to work designing the packaging of her socially conscious lipsticks. Her first product illustrated President Trump with his lips painted a classic shade of red. She asked customers to vote which organisation they would like 50 per cent of the profits to go towards.

To date, Katie has raised around $200,000 (over £155,000) for causes Trump has failed, including Planned Parenthood, victims of white nationalist violence in Charlottesville, Virginia, and families separated at the US-Mexico border.

When Brett Kavanaugh, a man who was nominated and later appointed to become a judge in the US's highest court, was accused of sexual assault, Katie launched a deep red lipstick and donated the proceeds to organisations working to end sexual violence. She did the same to combat similar allegations against movie producer Harvey Weinstein.

Katie is proof that it's possible for business owners to do the right thing. They've just got to want their product to give back.

KATIE

The first time I really understood that things were not right in the world was during the 2008 California state elections. I was 12 years old and Proposition 8 — a policy to keep California from recognising same sex marriages — was a huge nationwide controversy. I still remember being disheartened at listening to people argue about the basic human rights of others.

Watching Trump's inauguration gave me the same feeling. I talked to my friends about how we could do our bit. Eventually, we landed on this idea to somehow funnel money from people's everyday spending habits to the causes they really cared about. I'd recently read a statistic that claimed the average woman spent well over $15,000 (£12,000) on cosmetics during her lifetime. With this, my degree in packaging and printing technology, and my lifelong love of cosmetics in mind, I figured I'd give it a go.

The name Lipslut seemed to come out of nowhere and it stuck. I used Google to create a website and decided to take pre-orders for lipsticks to come up with the money for our first batch of products. To this day, I'm amazed that it worked!

I sometimes see huge multinational corporations bragging about the fact they've raised $100,000 (£80,000) for charity. Before Lipslut, I thought that was impressive. Now that I've been able to raise more than double that in just one year, I think other companies should be doing way more. By no means do I want to brag, but it's deeply unnerving that one 22-year-old girl with a couch and a laptop is outperforming billion-dollar companies. I think it's time that the corporate world steps up and that customers expect better.

The ultimate goal of Lipslut is to change the world one face at a time, and to create an empowering community of women. In many ways, the current Lipslut community has built a great foundation for this bold goal. Now we have to work harder to broaden our impact.

 ## GREAT THINGS NEVER HAPPEN ALONE.

Sure, I've hired a shipping company to send out orders but it's still largely just me working from my laptop. I'm sure I'm not the only one who would like to see the money they spend going towards organisations genuinely trying to make the world a better place.

With the amount of information almost everyone has at their fingertips, understanding problems and taking action towards solving them is easier than ever before. If you're truly passionate about something, there's always a way to make it work. Assume you know nothing, learn as much as you can, and always be the first to admit when you are wrong.

I often think of a quote from *Star Wars*: "Do or do not. There is no try." I have "tried" to do a million things in my life; and have been unsuccessful every single time. Lipslut is something I simply "did".

IF you'RE TRuLy PASSiONATE aBouT SOMETHiNG, THERE's aLWAYS A WaY To MAKE it WORK.

KATIE SONES

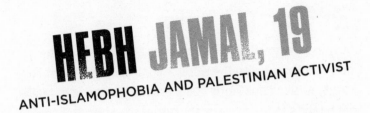

HEBH JAMAL, 19

ANTI-ISLAMOPHOBIA AND PALESTINIAN ACTIVIST

Being a Muslim Palestinian-American means Hebh Jamal has been asked lots of inappropriate questions, even when she was a child. At the age of 12, a teacher asked her what she thought of the fact that the leader of the Al-Qaeda terrorist organisation, Osama bin Laden, had been assassinated. At 15, a reporter requested that she shed light on her experience of being a young Muslim woman living in America. She was too young to remember the 9/11 terror attacks, but her words struck a chord with a lot of people.

She knows what it's like to be forced to make others feel comfortable around her and her religion, but her work aims to put an end to those feelings of fear and awkwardness. She doesn't want to be the poster girl for the female Muslim community, but she wants people of all faiths and identities to feel safe and have equal access to healthcare, education, and decent standards of living.

Hebh used her life experiences and her new audience to speak out, first appearing at a local school then organising walkouts protesting against Islamophobic attitudes, school segregation, and more. Each and every one of her efforts have brought hundreds of people together and kept them fighting for what they know is right.

HEBH

Living in a post-9/11 America shapes almost everything about how you interact with the world around you. My Palestinian identity is also constantly being erased by American media, which tends to focus on Israel, rather than how the conflict is affecting the lives of Palestinian people. All of this meant that I was politicised from a young age.

Before high school, I wasn't a big reader. But during my sophomore year, I started reading anything that was given to me. I learnt about different ideologies and political movements. I read about how civil rights authors and activists such as James Baldwin, Malcolm X and Martin Luther King didn't just get out there and protest. They listened and read and wrote first. Ninety-nine per cent of activism is hidden, behind-the-scenes stuff like this, but the one per cent, which involves gathering thousands of people, is the flashy part that everyone sees.

The things that people are fighting for now are not new problems, but people are speaking about them as if they are. I wanted to make people realise that Islamophobia, school segregation, and unequal healthcare aren't Donald Trump issues; they're historical American issues.

One protest did turn into an anti-Trump demonstration. But it was still a really amazing experience. I was on the train with thousands of students. Everyone started clapping and joining in with my chant. It's not a moment you get to live very often, but it showed the importance of protests. They get people talking; they can change minds.

I didn't want the protests to be just about me. If they were, what happens if I get run over by a bus? When a movement focuses on one person, there isn't a message. My faith has helped me shift the focus. Islam helps people create a community, but I've seen a community die when its leader isn't there anymore.

For a long time, everything I did was just like talking to a brick wall. It was really hard to try to bring about change and feel that the whole world was against me. One example is school segregation. New York City has one of the most segregated school systems in the country, which means that your ethnicity, your family income, and where you live can affect what school you go to and the educational opportunities that you receive. When I talked about the separation in New York City's school system, teachers would call me a bad student for wanting to destroy the system or say that it wasn't important. I couldn't wrap my head around the concept of turning against something that affects students, particularly students of colour from low-income communities.

But I helped establish an organisation and got a job writing policy for the school integration cause. There came a point where I realised I was no longer needed in the movement. I recently got an email saying that the framework I wrote is now Department of Education policy. I wasn't there when the policy was decided, but I definitely helped lead up to it.

Right now, I'm realising that it is difficult to openly practice your faith when integrating in to the culture of a country like the US. I constantly hear stories of how the FBI are knocking on my friends' doors just because they're involved in the mosque. So, I'm trying to understand what the role of Muslims is in countries that don't necessarily want us there; that believe that our faith opposes their Western values. My job as the youth-focused director of a Muslim organisation in New York City isn't to disprove that but to empower the next generation.

It's so important to **SURROUND YOURSELF** with intellectually **DRIVEN PEOPLE** that **CHALLENGE** you and make you think about the world **DIFFERENTLY**.

I value those conversations more than anything. And that's the essence of a movement. It's not about you, but about all the people you can impact.

If you are a member of the LGBTQ+ community (which stands for Lesbian, Gay, Bisexual, Transgender/ Transsexual, Queer plus other inclusive groups such as asexual and intersex), you will have undoubtedly experienced the challenges that come with opening your identity up to others. And if you're not, you will almost certainly be aware of the injustices that this community face.

The story of LGBTQ+ rights has been one of courage, bravery, and pride. For a long time, many LGBTQ+ communities were alienated and discriminated against. But now, in many places, those same communities are welcomed and also celebrated in pride marches, which take place across the globe every spring and summer. Their rights have also been protected with the passing of laws such as the UK's Equality Act (Sexual Orientations) Regulations which, in 2007, made it illegal to discriminate against someone because of their sexual orientation. (In 2010, the act also banned gender reassignment discrimination.) Or the fact that over 40 countries have criminalised homophobic hate crimes since 1990.

But unfortunately, there is still a way to go before full equality can be achieved. People still find themselves subjected to both physical and verbal abuse for their sexual orientation or gender identity. They may steer clear of certain crowds or areas to avoid harassment and often won't report incidents because they believe authorities have little interest in protecting them.

Being gay is also still illegal in 72 countries across the world, and eight of those countries still have the ability to punish homosexual relationships by death. Transgender people are discriminated against even more. Several countries strip them of their right to legally change their name and gender. And when they are allowed, they must go through an excruciatingly long process in order to "prove" themselves.

Ignorance is a large portion of the problem. As many trans people will tell you, fear breeds contempt. And when people don't understand something, they naturally become scared of it. Yet when we show and celebrate all sorts of identities, we see how multi-faceted and wonderful they make the world – and this can help banish those feelings of hate!

The people I'm about to introduce you to are doing just that – educating others about their identities and speaking face-to-face with politicians to encourage them to put protective laws in place. And it's not just up to the LGBTQ+ community itself to help. People who don't identify as LGBTQ+ can be equal allies and also do their part. You could start an app to help those in danger, you could promote inclusive literature and education, you could lobby your politicians for help, or you could simply raise awareness by retweeting the stories and campaigns of others.

The next few activists are proof that one small effort can affect many. Let them and their stories be your inspiration.

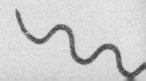

SAGE GRACE
DOLAN-SANDRINO, 18
ARTIST, TRANS RIGHTS ADVOCATE

A transgender person is someone whose true identity does not match the gender identity they were assigned at birth. Some people are assigned a male identity but know they are female; others are assigned a girl identity but identify as a boy. They often undergo a transition, which is the process that allows them to look on the outside how they feel on the inside. This can involve physical, social and psychological changes.

Unfortunately, transgender youths are often prevented from living life as their true selves. This is sometimes because their families and friends don't have the knowledge to deal with a transition in the right way. Or it could be the fault of schools who sometimes refuse to divert from rigid gender rules; for example, by blocking someone who identifies as a girl from using the female toilets. Sage Grace Dolan-Sandrino's childhood pain falls firmly into the latter category. Growing up in Maryland in the US, her mum was hugely supportive; some fellow school students less so. But school staff were the ones who really showed a lack of understanding.

So Sage Grace formed her own community and became involved in politics, advising politicians how they can help advance transgender rights in all parts of life. She has had her setbacks along the way but despite that, she has the drive needed to get things done. Whether it's by studying film to communicate trans stories to the public or pushing young people to vote for the future they want, she will not sit back and let other people take control of her life.

SAGE GRACE

I knew I was a girl before I could even express it. But I quickly learned that everyone else thought I was a boy. This meant that all of my best times living as a girl in those early years had to be somewhat secret and I could only wear the clothes I liked inside my house. It was rare for anyone to have the vocabulary or understanding of transgender kids back then.

In middle school (the school children in the US go to between primary and secondary), I discovered that there were other people like me and decided that I couldn't wait any longer to live publicly as my true self. The first day I stepped out of the house as a young woman and headed to the bus stop, I was both excited and scared. Unfortunately, it didn't exactly go smoothly – I was assaulted, denied use of the proper bathroom in school, and ridiculed. But I was finally myself.

My mum was supportive from the beginning, but it took my dad a little bit more time to understand my identity. By the time I reached high school and there was more publicity around the trans identity, as well as more resources available for families, my dad recognised me as his daughter.

I've always liked public speaking, writing, and telling stories. And I'm also a pretty determined person. But having to campaign for my right to be who I am forced me into activism. My first role was as a spokesperson for the organisations that had helped me with my transition. Through that, I met other people who offered me platforms to share my experience as a mixed race, black and Latinx (the gender neutral term for the Latin community) trans student. I got involved with institutions such as The White House's Initiative on Educational Excellence for African Americans and The Aspen Institute, and was soon published in the *Washington Post*, *Teen Vogue*, and *Vice*.

Myself, and a group of other trans students, also worked with the former US Education Secretary on transgender rights in public schools. Two years later, I was called to confront the new Education Secretary, who was appointed by President Donald Trump, in the same boardroom as she removed those rights. It proved that Trump's regime is trying to legislate us out of existence.

My transness has presented me with many difficulties, yet I've also had the privilege of having academic and medical help as well as support from my family.

It's my responsibility to use those privileges to FIGHT FOR OTHERS.

Many trans teens grow up in unsupportive environments where it can be dangerous for them to come out. Black and Latina(x) transgender women specifically face even more danger. We are criminalised and forced in to unsafe situations in order to afford costly and often unreachable medical care, housing, and employment opportunities. We suffer from poverty at greater rates than the general population, and we also face severe mental-health crises when we aren't supported.

I am a transgender woman of colour and this political identity means that I fight for the cause every day just by living. But my studies are currently taking up most of my time. I'm studying film so that I can be the author of my own future. So that I can bring a sense of truth to the stories of girls and women like me.

Not all change-making has to be public. If public speaking doesn't appeal to you, write articles and find an online community. If you're an artist, choreograph or sing. There is no limit to the mediums that can be used to change our communities.

We are the most diverse, queer, and progressive of any generation yet. We know how to organise and how to use technology to create and communicate. We can transform oppression into liberation. We will not be silenced or defeated.

COREY MAISON, 17

TRANSGENDER YOUTH CAMPAIGNER

When Corey Maison was younger, she loved playing with dolls and painting her nails, but only inside the safety of her own home. Why? Because Corey was born as a male and yet identified as a female.

One day, her mum showed her a documentary about transgender teenager Jazz Jennings. Corey was relieved. Here was proof that she was just a girl, and not abnormal like other children had made her feel.

Corey's transition was first documented by her mum. A video of her being presented with her first batch of female hormones has now been watched over seven million times. Corey then felt brave enough to share her story alone.

She posted the typical selfies of any teenage girl but teamed them with captions, offering honesty and encouragement to other kids like her. She helped her state create better protection for transgender students in schools and, when Donald Trump was elected as President of the United States, she posted a heartfelt video urging trans people to stick together, rise up and keep championing what they believe in. Her openness even encouraged her own mum to transition and live life as a man.

She dreams of a TV career and becoming the first transgender Victoria's Secret model. Pushing yourself in to that kind of limelight takes immense courage, no matter who you are. Then again, Corey has already proven herself in that department.

COREY

I spent a lot of my life questioning why I was here and why I was so angry at the world. It was extremely difficult, but not as difficult as living a lie.

People outside of the trans community often don't understand how long the transitioning process actually takes. It doesn't happen overnight; it takes years of being closely followed by a medical team before you're even allowed to start taking cross-sex hormones. I had to wait over two years before my doctor could prescribe me oestrogen. It seemed like a lifetime, but I can't describe how it felt to look in the mirror and finally see my true self.

I lost some friends when I transitioned. My mum told me that they weren't really my friends to begin with if they couldn't stick by my side when I needed them, and my mum was 100 per cent right. But being bullied will affect me for the rest of my life. Yes, I was able to overcome it and am now a stronger person, but those awful words and feelings are still with me every day.

It breaks my heart that not all trans people have a huge support system like I do. Mine includes my mum who has now transitioned to male. We all still call him Mum which is confusing for some, but it's what works best for our family.

After my hormone video went viral, I realised I had a platform to be able to help other trans kids. The state I live in, Michigan, previously had no guidelines to keep LGBTQ+ kids safe in schools, so schools were free to decide if trans girls had the right to use the girls' bathroom or the right to play on the girls' sports teams. When I was invited to give my input on Department of Education policy to stop this, I accepted immediately. I was there when the votes were cast and will never forget how much my hands were shaking. When the policy won, I gave my mum the tightest hug and we cried tears of joy together.

Knowing I was a **PART OF HISTORY** being made felt like such an incredible honour.

It can feel bizarre that thousands of people see in to my life, but it's also really cool. I get hundreds of messages from people online. Sometimes they're from random people who say I have opened up their eyes and hearts. The best messages are from kids who tell me that they are still alive because of me.

I do occasionally get hateful messages on social media or mailed to my house. People are often scared of what they don't understand and it's easy to turn that fear into anger.

The way I cope with it is to tell myself that there is so much more love in this world than hate, and that love will always win.

It's my goal to make this world a better place. I hope to see equality for everyone and hope to see the suicide rate from transgender youths drop to that of the general population.

People need to know that they are perfect exactly the way they are, and that saying your feelings out loud, rather than keeping them bottled up inside, can be such a relief. If you are trans, find someone you can trust to talk to: a friend, teacher, counsellor, anyone. It's not an easy road but it sure is a beautiful one.

PEOPLE ARE
SCARED
OF WHAT
THEY DON'T
UNDERSTAND.

COREY MAISON

LILY MADIGAN, 21

POLITICAL TRANS ACTIVIST

When Lily Madigan came out as transgender, she was determined to live as her true self even though she felt her school in Kent, UK did not accept her. For example, one day when she turned up wearing a girls' uniform to school, Lily said she was sent home. On other occasions she had to fight to use the female toilet, as well as be called by her chosen name. But with the help of a lawyer, she argued for the rights she felt she was entitled to as a transgender student.

This was the beginning of Lily's political career. In November 2017, she became the first transgender person to be elected as a Labour Party women's officer. She fought for the rights of all women and received malicious abuse in return. But she also built up an online community focused on helping people like her through difficult times.

Trans people are still seriously under-represented in society, especially politics. But with Lily's efforts, which focus on reversing the damage caused by uncaring governments and teaming up with the likes of Puma and *Teen Vogue* to highlight the importance of trans visibility, that will be a thing of the past.

LILY

I came out as trans via Facebook. All my friends were very supportive, but my family weren't, and still aren't that supportive even today. Years later, I came out as gay on Twitter. The response was largely positive, although some transphobic and homophobic people still sent me abuse.

This abuse is a big part of social media and is something that should be taken a lot more seriously. I try not to think too much about the negatives and

keep on **CAMPAIGNING** for what I believe in, in the **HOPE** that one day this kind of abuse won't even exist.

When I came out as transgender, I felt that I was treated terribly by my school administration. It was a horrific time in my life. I wanted to be treated like a female student. It was important to me that I could use the correct spaces, wear a girl's uniform and be referred to by my chosen name with the correct pronoun. But no matter how much I challenged my school, I felt they did not accommodate my needs.

I felt like legal action was my only option, so as soon as I turned 18, I saved up, went to London, and visited a number of law firms. Eventually, I found a firm that asked my school to uphold my rights under the UK Equality Act 2010. The school apologised for causing me any unintentional hurt, said transgender issues were important to them and agreed to treat me as I requested. My case has since certainly made it easier for other trans students but it's important we continue to speak up when trans people are facing inequality.

Politics wasn't even something I paid attention to before the school incident. But the Labour Party introduced the Equality Act that enabled me to argue against my former school and was a big factor in why I joined the party too. I chose to run for the women's officer position because I'm very aware that my mistreatment is largely because I'm a trans woman. For example, a trans boy wearing trousers wouldn't be seen as a problem but it's the reverse for a trans girl wearing a skirt.

It was a great feeling when I was awarded the role. It also made me feel accepted and acknowledged for the person that I am. So far, I have managed to achieve a few things – I helped protect refuge funding, spoke to my local community about the suffragette movement, and wrote and passed motions (which are proposals that are put forward for a debate or vote in UK Parliament) for decriminalising abortions in Northern Ireland and supporting women who are making that choice.

Starting campaigns is hard. I'm working to get one off the ground called #AskYouthToStand. My aim is to call out the lack of young people in Parliament and to encourage them to consider standing. Under 30s make up less than two per cent of MPs here. It's a depressing statistic but it explains why our priorities are so often ignored.

Creating a movement involves choosing what you're passionate about, going to events, and speaking up when you're comfortable to make others passionate too. Those from marginalised groups are just as capable of making that change as anybody else.

I personally have a lot of aspirations. I want us all to be able to get on the housing ladder and for that housing to be of a good quality. When we are ill, I want us all to have adequate local health services that are going to be able to treat us well and quickly. And when we fall on hard times, as so many of us do, I want those centres and staff to be able to look after everyone. My ultimate political goal is for all of us to feel able to aspire to success and, crucially, for no group to get left behind.

Find the
things you're
passionate about
and research them.

Go to events
and speak up
to incite that
passion in other
people.

LILY MADIGAN

AMELIA ROSKIN-FRAZEE, 22

INCLUSIVITY CAMPAIGNER, FOUNDER OF THE MAKE IT SAFE PROJECT

Books have the ability to teach you about the world, about who you are as a person, and about who you could be in years to come. When Amelia Roskin-Frazee was growing up, she didn't see herself in any of her library books. Figuring that this wasn't just a local issue, she began to create boxes, filling them with books about sexual orientation and gender identity. Each box is then donated to schools, youth shelters, and juvenile detention centres across the US.

The Make It Safe Project found its official name when Amelia was 14 and it hasn't stopped growing since. Her initial goal of giving over 100 thousand youths the resources they need has been met, and she has even expanded abroad to countries that are also lacking in the inclusivity department.

Although Amelia is grateful for the books that already exist, she wants to create more. That's why she organises a writing scholarship each year, encouraging anyone who identifies as LGBTQ+ to express their feelings through literature. Eventually, the submissions will be compiled in to one big book and included in every box she sends out.

If that wasn't inspiring enough, Amelia also works alongside GLSEN, an organisation promoting inclusivity in schools, and campaigns against sexual violence at her university. All of that sounds exhausting, and it is. Even if she has to take a break every now and then, Amelia knows that her vision of a discrimination-free world is just within reach. All she, and you, need to keep on doing is reaching for it.

AMELIA

I'll admit that I grew up in a bit of a bubble. I went to my first Pride Parade when I was two and have always been fortunate to be surrounded by supportive friends and family. It wasn't until I got older that I saw the many problems facing queer people and survivors of violence.

When I came out to my classmates online, I realised the resources I wanted on being queer did not exist at my school. I also learned that there was a lack of LGBTQ+-inclusive literature for teens in general. So, I started a Gay-Straight Alliance at my school and founded The Make It Safe Project. So far, I've given more than 130 thousand teens access to books in 26 states and abroad.

When I started Columbia University, I was already a survivor of sexual violence. But I was assaulted again on campus during my first semester. I was frustrated with the lack of resources for survivors and how the resources that did exist were often inadequate and discriminatory against the LGBTQ+ community and people of colour.

One of my biggest accomplishments was getting the university to add gender-based harassment to its misconduct policy. This means that students can report people who have done things like threatening to 'out', or actually 'outing', someone as queer or trans. And I'm also really proud of managing to get a box of books into the state of Utah, which has a reputation for being a highly conservative and religious place. This is a stereotype but sending a box of LGBTQ+ books there was honestly really difficult to accomplish.

Despite these successes, I have had moments of questioning my participation in activism — especially after being assaulted twice in my first year at university. It was definitely hard to find the motivation to go back to advocating for others when I was barely emotionally together myself. The idea of walking across campus with LGBTQ+-related books terrified me and holding a megaphone made my arm shake. Thankfully, I've found

ACTIVISM can be a great way to channel PAIN into something POSITIVE and PRODUCTIVE.

When in doubt, I always think of an amazing quote by writer and activist Audre Lorde: "Caring for myself is not self-indulgence, it is self-preservation, and that is an act of political warfare."

It's so true. Talking non-stop about violence and discrimination is exhausting. If you don't focus on your health, you will experience burnout. So, find fun events to do with your fellow activists (I personally recommend frequenting your local cat café, if you have one), check in with one another, and don't be afraid to take a step back if you get overwhelmed.

There's still a lot we need to address inside the LGBTQ+ community itself, namely that it centres white cisgender people (that's people who identify as the sex they were born as) and sacrifices others. But all of us can help the community by focusing on things such as violence against trans women of colour, imprisonment, immigration, homelessness, inclusive sex education in schools, and equal access to healthcare. (You'll notice that these revolve around helping a larger part of the community, rather than things such as legalising marriage, which only help a select few people.)

A decade from now, I hope the mainstream queer rights movement allows people of colour a chance to raise their voice and that it delves into deeper issues that discriminate against certain groups. One such issue is how the criminal justice system fails trans people by sometimes suspending medical treatment and placing them in prisons that don't correspond to their gender identity. I hope we can all focus on working with others, rather than profiting from them and their experiences.

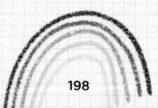

ELLEN JONES, 20

LGBTQ+ AND MENTAL HEALTH CAMPAIGNER

At the age of 14, Ellen Jones came out. It took a toll on her mental health, but her ability to educate herself about sexuality, gender, and disability, and fight for better rights for all has transformed her in to an award-winning activist.

Ellen first acted after seeing how little people knew of the many issues faced by the LGBTQ+ community and how quickly hard-won rights could be snatched away. She helped her school tackle inequality, trained as a campaigner with LGBTQ+ organisation Stonewall, and became a supportive face on YouTube, allowing people to ask difficult questions and a diverse group of LGBTQ+ individuals to answer.

Some of her campaigning, the reasons she was named Stonewall's Young Campaigner of the Year in 2017 and awarded the first Generation Change EMA by MTV in late 2018, is public. Some of it is carried out behind closed doors. You won't see or hear of the work Ellen has done behind the scenes in the media to stop discriminatory content from ever seeing the light of day, but it's very much there.

Summing a person like Ellen Jones up isn't easy. She's more than open about the ups and downs of being an activist and talks about the issues but doesn't pretend to have all the answers. So perhaps "refreshingly real" would do her justice.

ELLEN

I am an openly queer, autistic, bipolar young woman with opinions. I only started seriously campaigning about two years ago and was astounded by how much I could achieve, even if it was just within my small local bubble. My obsession with Doctor Who was a major driving force. The Doctor is a character running around the universe, being kind, offering hope and helping out where they can. I idolised that.

I first came out when I was 14. Since then, I have come out approximately 5,059,591 times because heteronormativity, which is the belief that being heterosexual is the 'norm', means that I have to out myself every time I meet a new person or enter a new space. Coming out at such a young age presented a lot of challenges. People would constantly invalidate me and I was horrendously cyberbullied by many of those closest to me, which had a fairly catastrophic impact on my mental health.

I didn't know I could exist as a **GAY PERSON**, let alone be **HAPPY** or **SUCCESSFUL**.

I still struggle with that from time to time but having the support of Stonewall has been invaluable. In 2016, I completed the organisation's Young Campaigners programme which essentially trains you up and then provides support whilst you develop and deliver campaigns in your local community. A year later, Stonewall named me their Young Campaigner of the Year for tackling LGBTQ+ inequality in schools and online.

I also have my own YouTube channel. I've always watched a lot of social justice content and wanted to start talking about the issues that affected my community. Queeries is the series I'm most proud of. Each video sees me and a guest answering questions about being LGBTQ+ that have been sent in by the audience. It's an opportunity for us to speak openly about issues that may challenge assumptions or move beyond the typical LGBTQ+ narratives. LGBTQ+ people are constantly being asked invasive questions and, while I think discussion is an important part of education, it's the LGBTQ+ people who should control when, where, how, and if those discussions happen.

As a queer disabled woman, everything I make will be politicised. But I never set out to be considered as an activist; I'm often simply defending the right to just be me. It's necessary and worthwhile but I'd be lying if I said it wasn't truly exhausting.

It doesn't help that being LGBTQ+ in this climate feels like being constantly on edge because those in power still have the ability to make people's identities illegal. There has also arguably been a rapid rise in fascism across the globe. This type of thinking believes a country is more important than the individual people living in it, and is terrifying to watch. It's hard to know how to fight all of that, but we can and we will. There is no one size fits all solution. But researching issues and listening to and supporting different people dealing with different challenges are good places to start.

I think it's also important to learn that being a respectable and attractive young woman isn't the be all and end all. Young women are often taught that their worth is defined by how they are perceived by others and are often judged by the way they look. But I believe those expectations are just designed to keep us in line. You should determine what you think of yourself. That way, any criticism you get from people will hurt a lot less.

You don't have to ignore criticism or be unkind, but don't hide away parts of your identity for other people's benefit. I don't, and it's my biggest achievement. It's what made people tell me that I have given them permission to be themselves and to feel like they can exist as nothing but their whole self.

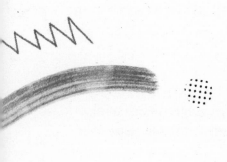

AMANDA SOUTHWORTH, 17

CODER AND APP DEVELOPER, FOUNDER OF ASTRA LABS

Technology saved Amanda Southworth's life. That's not an overdramatic statement, but a true one. Throughout school, she suffered with a number of mental health issues, but found a way to cope after falling head over heels for robotics. She taught herself how to code and develop apps, eventually coming up with an idea that aimed to help people like her.

AnxietyHelper officially launched in 2015. Designed to give guidance and support to those suffering from anxiety, depression and more, it created a global community of people that had once suffered in silence.

Two years later, real threats to the safety of the LGBTQ+ community emerged. Amanda knew another app was needed. She named it Verena. It provides details of nearby police stations, hospitals, and shelters in the United States, and allows users to quickly alert family or friends if they are in need.

Amanda saw so many positive sides to technology that she started her own company. Astra Labs is a joint venture with a friend and aims to develop free, accessible, and life-changing apps to help those who feel lost and alone. Managing to impress the CEO of Apple and getting her apps on to more than 80 thousand devices means that Amanda is leading the new generation of technology bosses. Whatever she comes up with next, she is hellbent on transforming Silicon Valley into a place of help, not profit.

AMANDA

Growing up was just flat out awful for me. I have complex post-traumatic stress disorder (C-PTSD), and from fifth until eleventh grade, wasn't in a good place with my family or mental health.

But when I reached sixth grade, I enrolled in a robotics class. It was love at first sight, like one of those corny scenes in a movie where the two characters look at each from across the room and swoon. In my case, it wasn't two people, but a person and a computer. The class taught me the basics of programming but I would spend hours reading Wikipedia pages and college textbooks to learn more.

Some people's platforms are Instagram and YouTube or even art and make-up. But for me, it was my apps. Whenever I see something that desperately needs to be changed, I create an app for it.

'BE THE PERSON YOU NEEDED WHEN YOU WERE YOUNGER,'

is the saying I now live by. I realised I wanted to create a support system for others, so they wouldn't have to search for a reason to live as long as I did. And that's exactly what my first app, AnxietyHelper, does.

When I was working on it, my schedule was insane. I would wake up at 5 a.m. to work on the app, go to school from 7:30 a.m. until 3 p.m., do homework until 6 p.m., eat dinner, and then continue working on the app until 2 or 3 a.m. I only got around 17 downloads on the first day, and every single one was from my friends. You could tell that no one thought it would become this giant monster that consumes every aspect of my life. But it has. I've even had people recognise me in public and tell me how much it has helped them.

My next app was much more political. Most of my friendship group is made up of minorities. So when the 2016 presidential election came around, it was scary. We had elected a president who, in my and other people's opinion, declared himself anti-LGBTQ+ and anti-immigrants, with his actions hurting many minorities.

At lunch, me and my friends were sitting in an empty classroom, talking about our fears. That fuelled me into tackling the one thing close to my heart: LGBTQ+ rights. Verena launched in 2017. The name means "protector" in German. Everything in the app is designed to prevent and help with hate crimes and abuse. Just like AnxietyHelper, people loved it and told me how much of a difference it's made to their lives.

At the moment, I think that technology is being used to solve the wrong problems. Entire companies are built to improve things that aren't actually broken. For example, there are numerous products that make your home smarter but there isn't a fully accessible app to help with mental health or disability. My organisation, Astra Labs, does the complete opposite. It is a software development company that will house the best innovators and activists in the world. Of course, it isn't going to fix everything immediately, but a journey always starts with a first step.

It's important to start that journey as soon as possible and insert seeds of tolerance and diversity in the next generation. If we ever want things to get better, we have to fight for the change that we want to see. It will not be handed to us. Right now, you have a voice. Use it before you can't.

ELLA FIELDS, 15

FILMMAKER

You can create a community in so many ways: through public speaking, through writing, or, like Ella Fields did, through film. Ella's films are short, no longer than ten minutes, but boy do they make an impact.

It could be because she explores everything from gender stereotypes and LGBTQ+ emotions to gun violence. It could be because she doesn't exclude anyone and invites those who have an opposing view to ask questions and take part in the conversation. Whatever her secret is, Ella's success cannot be ignored. Millions have watched her films, awards have been won, and countless people have told her how seeing their story play out on the screen has helped them mentally and emotionally.

Hard-hitting work isn't her only passion. She has also become a recognisable face on YouTube, posting videos of herself giving advice on how to come out to your parents, how to start a new school, and even how to direct your own films.

Revealing your inner self and voicing your opinions can be frightening. Ella knows exactly what that anxiety is like. But she wants people to see that showing your unique perspective to others is one way to a better world. Some may not like it, but many, many will.

ELLA

I think it's important to try to find the beauty in things.

★ **SOCIAL MEDIA** can separate us, but it can also **BRING US TOGETHER** in ways never possible before.

Living in Los Angeles, I've been very lucky to be surrounded by open-minded people. I know other parts of my country, and even the world, aren't as free-thinking. With YouTube, I have been able to reach people from all over the world.

I've always been in to film. When I was six, my dad brought me and my sister a cheap flip camera for my sister to play around with. We'd film everything, and I mean everything. That led to me applying for a film-focused middle school. There, I learned how to write, direct, film, edit, and design props and costumes; it was a one woman show. Every time I produced something, my passion would grow.

I have three short films that I am super proud of. I created *Stereo* towards the end of my eighth-grade year. Being a young girl obsessed with *Transformers* and sports, I thought that basic gender stereotypes were meaningless, so I made a film where they were reversed. Finding teenage boys who would wear dresses was difficult, but the reaction to it has been beyond incredible; it's now on its way to seven million views on YouTube.

People told me that it has really changed their perspective on life, which makes me feel like the art I create actually matters.

Bubble Gum, however, was my biggest passion project. I'm a big advocate for how sexuality is such a fluid thing and how nothing is ever black and white. I was coming to certain realisations about my own sexuality and wanted to showcase what an incredibly confusing time it could be. I filmed the entire thing in one weekend. Again, the film gained quite a bit of recognition on YouTube and has also won numerous awards. Girls in particular have said that it helped them come to terms with their sexuality, come out to people around them, or even make films of their own.

Voices was another project I felt very strongly about. I've experienced a shooting at my school, so the topic of gun control hits very close to home. The response to my film on the controversial issue hasn't been completely positive, but I was expecting that. It's been intriguing to hear everyone's interpretations of the situation, even if I don't agree with them.

I think it's difficult to comprehend just how many things are wrong with the world. People are being shown that discrimination is okay and the people in power are trying to separate us. That's why I don't just want to tell any old story. I want to tell stories that matter; stories that help people cope.

It takes a lot of courage to create something, let alone share it with anyone, but know that your opinion matters and that it's okay to speak relentlessly and fearlessly. If you stay true to your individual beliefs and morals, you will truly make a difference. Trust me, I know.

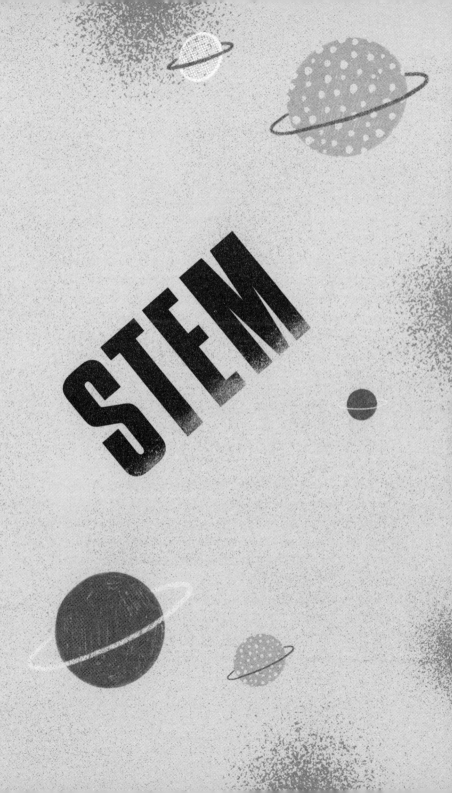

Science, technology, engineering, and maths (or STEM, as it's more commonly known) is all around us. It's responsible for almost everything we own and do, from the phone you carry around with you 24/7 to the biological reason why you love a certain food and can't stand others. Looking back in the history books, it's easy to think that all of the achievements in these fields were carried out by men. After all, how many female scientists or engineers can you name?

Struggling to think of even five? You're not alone. Throughout the ages, the work of women has often been forgotten or disregarded. Here's just a few examples. Microbiologist Esther Lederberg carried out vital genetics research that helped her husband win a Nobel Prize in 1958, Lise Meitner's nuclear physics findings in the first half of the 20th century were rarely mentioned by her celebrated male colleagues, and three NASA mathematicians – Katherine Johnson, Dorothy Vaughan and Mary Jackson – were unknown to the wider world until their stories became the plot of a Hollywood film.

But the following young women are making sure no female inventor, scientist, engineer or mathematician, is ever forgotten again. They have battled their way to get a seat at the table and are ensuring that no other girl with a knack for problem-solving gets left behind.

Just like their overlooked female predecessors, these great minds see a problem and seek to fix it through any means possible. Some of them fell into STEM by accident; others were encouraged by their equally inquisitive families. But all have a passion to solve global issues, both large and small.

Most have experienced being the only girl in their STEM class and have many tales of not being taken seriously because of their gender or age. Luckily, that didn't deter them. If it did, the world wouldn't have been introduced to inventions that could solve the global food and energy crisis or even just the knowledge that young women deserve equal opportunities!

So, whether you want to become an active member of The STEAM Squad (the "A" has recently been introduced and stands for the arts) or just want to take inspiration from their brilliance, know that you are welcome. By working together, women can think up all kinds of inventions and empower themselves to work in any field they wish.

Why not summon up the courage to enrol in that class you've always dreamed of taking or create that gadget that's been filling your dreams for months. You'll never know what you can achieve until you at least try ...

TAYLOR RICHARDSON, 15

ASTRONAUT-IN-TRAINING, DIVERSITY AND STEM ADVOCATE

Only three black women have made it into space. Taylor Richardson is aiming to be the fourth. But she doesn't want to make the flight path alone; she's bringing thousands of girls of colour along with her.

Taylor realised that literature can inspire us all and so she set up her 'Take Flight with a Book' initiative, which saw her deliver more than five thousand books to children across Florida. That scored her an invite to watch *Hidden Figures,* the real-life story of three African American women who were overlooked in NASA's history, at the White House alongside former First Lady Michelle Obama.

The movie inspired Taylor. She knew other girls had to see what was possible. A few months down the line and she had raised $18,000 (almost £14,500) to send girls in her local area to watch the film. Another of Taylor's crowdfunders saw a thousand young people gifted with tickets to watch another diverse piece of cinema, *A Wrinkle in Time*. Taylor herself raised $50,000 (almost £44,000) and saw her efforts matched by Oprah Winfrey. People everywhere were so inspired by her

commitment that they launched their own fundraisers in her honour.

Now the subject of her very own documentary, Taylor, or Astro StarBright as she is known online, is set to be remembered in the history books as a young woman who didn't let a lack of resources stop her from giving back, or a lack of representation halt her rise into the stratosphere.

TAYLOR

At night, I used to lie in my yard and look up at the stars thinking about what was out there. Then I read Dr Mae Jemison's book, *Find Where The Wind Goes*, and learned about being an astronaut. I attended various space camps and launch bases to learn as much as possible about the field, but I wanted to see more people that looked like me in the industry.

Books allowed me to take flight toward anything that I could imagine, and both my mum and grandma have always taught me to help others and give back. With both of these feelings in mind, I realised that literacy could be the gateway to success. So, I set up my own book drives to help other kids take flight towards their own dreams and aspirations.

After winning the Champion of Service Award in Florida, I got to visit the White House and see a screening of *Hidden Figures* with Michelle Obama and the film's cast and crew. It was the first time I had seen an African American woman

in a meaningful STEM role in the mainstream media. That's what sparked the idea to raise money for screenings that would engage young women and people of colour in the opportunities that STEM could offer.

My campaigns inspired others and ultimately raised over $100,000 (approximately £80,000) to fund screenings in 72 cities around the world. I never thought I would raise that much, but being able to let thousands of young people see these movies left me with a very good feeling. It was unbelievable that even celebrities like Taraji P. Henson, Janelle Monae, Ava DuVernay, Storm Reid, JJ Abrams, Chris Pine, and Oprah Winfrey supported and donated to my cause.

My nickname StarBright is no longer about a little nine year old who was fascinated by the stars and the unknown. It now reminds me to shine my light in honour of those who came before me so that I could have a better life, to shine bright for those who are walking with me so we can fight to keep our place and purpose in this world, and for those who will walk after me to know that the battle is never-ending but hopefully getting easier.

I'm a black girl who has ADHD and is being raised by a low-income single parent, so I still experience many of the same struggles and pressures as my peers. The difference is I don't allow them to affect my overall goal of being the best I can be. If I'm being bullied, I learn that it's just words. If my mum can't afford something, I just have to go without it. I'm being Abundantly Different and Happily Divine, and know that my path is not limited but limitless.

I hope the ways I've decided to combat my struggles can help people understand their power and see the humanity in others. All I want is to continue to keep that door open and that seat at the table warm so that other young people can follow my lead.

HANNAH HERBST, 18
SCIENTIST AND INVENTOR

Letter writing may be a dying art but it was this that gave Hannah Herbst her scientific break. When her Ethiopian pen pal explained that she was living without electricity and clean drinking water, Hannah knew she had the skills to help.

Hannah lives in Florida, a place almost entirely surrounded by water. Conveniently, 40 per cent of the world's population lives within roughly an hour's drive (100 kilometres) of the coast. Putting two and two together, she decided to solve both the energy and water crisis in one swift go.

A few months of solid work later and her device was complete. BEACON – which stands for Bringing Electricity Access To Countries Through Ocean Energy – features a propeller powered by ocean currents. This connects to a hydroelectric generator, converting energy into usable electricity. If scaled up, the invention could charge as much as three car batteries in less than an hour and purify water too.

This has earned Hannah many awards; America's Top Young Scientist being one of the most impressive. But her research hasn't stopped there. She is now exploring many possibilities including how shark skin could be used in medicine and how to better identify hazardous chemicals in the air. Hoping to inspire generations to come, she's a vitally important part of a community that will solve our planetary problems one way or another.

HANNAH

All most children know of science is what they have had to memorise from textbooks. Even I thought the field was dull. That changed in the summer before seventh grade when my dad introduced me to engineering through a STEM camp. Needless to say, I was a bit uncomfortable to be the only girl in camp alongside 40 boys. But that week completely shifted my perspective.

I realised the opportunity to succeed in science extended far beyond receiving high marks in an exam. Problem-solving through engineering became my passion and, that autumn, I joined every robotics club that my school had to offer.

During that year, I received a newsletter describing how my pen pal Ruth, who lives in Sub-Saharan Africa, was living in energy poverty without stable access to electricity. I felt burdened that other students my age lacked the basic resources that I had at my fingertips and felt a responsibility to act.

I was fishing with my family when inspiration struck. We were turning through a narrow stretch of water and I saw a large boat being turned by the current. I realised the current generated a huge amount of kinetic force and that this force could potentially be converted into usable electricity for those in need.

Over the next four years, I used this theory to develop a simple solution to the energy poverty crisis. Maths and science do not come easy to me; I had to spend hours learning principles so that I could apply them to my research.

And throughout the process, I learned far more from the failures that came with innovation than I did from the immediate successes. One example: I tested a prototype in my community swimming pool and it shattered in to pieces. But with the support and encouragement from mentors at my school, I finally developed a working prototype. In the field of engineering, we call this "proof of concept".

The fact that scientists and engineers are able to build upon what exists and make it even better is one of the many exciting aspects of discovery, so BEACON remains a model for others to use and improve. My hope is that people will use my design to develop more efficient methods of gathering energy from moving bodies of water.

I was recognised by Discovery Education and 3M as America's Top Young Scientist and by *Forbes* on its 30 under 30 list, and have presented at the White House Science Fair and the United Nations. Though each of these were exciting, the platform that it provided to inspire other young girls to pursue their passions was even more sensational for me. It led to mentoring opportunities for young girls at schools as well as the development of programmes to teach students living at the margins of life about robotics concepts that they probably would never have been exposed to.

All scientists begin in a lab with a mentor. All scientists have the potential to solve global-scale issues that could save lives. That's what I intend to keep doing for the rest of my life.

Nobody likes to **FAIL**. However, the
GREATEST SCIENTIFIC DISCOVERIES
of our world were a result of failures.

The key is to learn from them. We young women have much to offer, and by chasing our passions we can change the world.

KARI LAWLER, 15

TECHNOLOGY ENTREPRENEUR, FOUNDER OF LAWLER INDUSTRIES AND YOUTH4AI

It took Kari Lawler only a week to create something that could have rivalled Apple's Siri and Amazon's Alexa. Her digital assistant, Infinity, used artificial intelligence (AI) to answer questions. Unlike some people who are worried about how clever this kind of technology could become, Kari sees it as a way to help.

At the age of 14, Kari became the youngest person to secure a place on a campus for founders of start-up companies in Birmingham, UK. She has since been awarded for her outstanding contribution to her hometown. In 2018, she won the UK Space SatelLife Challenge; a competition held by the UK Space Agency that gives young people the chance to broadcast their ideas on how space satellites can be used to improve life. Her proposal unsurprisingly used AI.

She has also launched a scheme, Youth4AI, which teaches young people from all backgrounds what AI is and how they can use it to build the future. She aims to not only educate but also offer career advice and hold events for children who are intrigued by the ever-changing world of technology.

Kari is one of the AI world's youngest advocates and urges young people to achieve their dreams, no matter what challenges they face. She has personal experience of that particular struggle. Her autism diagnosis meant she found it hard to find a school that would give her a place. However, she strove to educate herself. And look where she is now.

KARI

Artificial intelligence is a very difficult term to explain. But I would define it as a machine that shows human-level intelligence. This definition is what researchers call 'General AI' and is currently what we can only dream of achieving.

However, what we have and use today is 'Narrow AI'. This mainly uses a technique called 'Machine Learning', which is where a machine is trained to understand huge amounts of data and then taught to complete a very specific task based on this. While this technology is producing some pretty amazing results (even proving better than humans at some tasks), the reality is we are still a long way from reaching anything comparable to human-level general intelligence.

It's rather ironic that I grew up in a house filled with computers and technology, but never really took an interest in them until I watched a documentary on chatbots a few years ago. That sparked my interest in AI and started my incredible journey. What really surprised me when I started out was the amount of free online courses that I could find to teach myself. I took as many of them as I could, including some from the top universities in the world such as Stanford and MIT.

My first hurdle was overcoming fear of the unknown. But I put those fears aside and just went for it. To my amazement, research and lots of trial and error allowed me to hack together my first — and very simple — chatbot! While Infinity was a great learning experience that got me noticed, I've now moved on to bigger projects. After talking to a lot of young people at events, I found that there was a lack of understanding of artificial intelligence. This was partly due to over-hyping and misinformation and negativity around AI in the media. To address this, I started an AI youth programme aimed at 13 to 25 year olds. Youth4AI has two missions. Firstly, to educate young people about what AI is and how it will play a major part in our future lives. Secondly, to provide young people with the technical skills needed to have a career in AI.

I've spoken in schools and seen that girls still have a misguided perception that technology is a boy's subject that heavily focuses on computers and coding. To fix this, schools and the curriculum need to showcase the varied roles available in the tech industry like neuroscientists and psychologists. Those kinds of people are highly sought after in the AI field.

When I first started on this journey, I thought it would be great to take a similar path to technology entrepreneur Elon Musk by starting and selling companies and growing to be the biggest provider of AI in the world. I realise that was overly ambitious but hey, a girl can dream! After a couple of years in the industry, I now seem to be moving towards helping to teach my generation, and the generations that will come afterwards, the knowledge needed to thrive in an AI-dominated future.

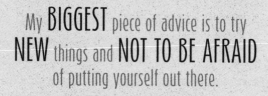

My **BIGGEST** piece of advice is to try **NEW** things and **NOT TO BE AFRAID** of putting yourself out there.

This is especially true in STEM where there are so many online resources to learn from and an amazing community that will always be there to support you.

ALYSSA CARSON, 17

TRAINEE ASTRONAUT

In 2033, the estimated year of the first manned mission to Mars, Alyssa is willing to leave her family, friends, and entire planet behind. With the help of her dad, Bert, she has travelled around the world training how to be an astronaut. She has been to NASA's space camps countless times, passed space-related courses intended for people several years older than her, and graduated from the super intense Advanced PoSSUM Academy. She knows how to deal with spacesuits, G-forces, decompression and microgravity, and can speak several languages including Mandarin.

It's safe to say that Alyssa is pretty well prepared to go anywhere in space, but she dreams of reaching one planet in particular. If selected for that mission to Mars, she will spend a few years living on the faraway planet and getting to know its harsh climates. She will grow food, perform daily experiments, and look for those all-important signs of life. At the end of it, she hopes to have found another home for the human race.

With ambitions to be the youngest person to fly in to space, Alyssa has attracted the attention of several rocket companies manned by people much older than her. But, right now, she enjoys spending time with other young girls and encourages them to take on the male-dominated science industry in any way possible.

You don't have to be willing to give your life for your passion like Alyssa, but a little dedication is all it takes to get to the top.

ALYSSA

Growing up, I was into all the things you would expect a little girl to be into. I loved Disney Princesses, the colour pink, and Barbie dolls. When I was three years old, I was watching an episode of *The Backyardigans*. It's a cartoon where these characters go on imaginary adventures in their backyard. The one I was watching saw the characters go to Mars. I wanted to go with them, so I asked my dad if it was possible.

He told me everything he knew about the moon landing and told me I could do anything I wanted to. So I told him that I wanted to be an astronaut. I think he figured I would just change my mind the next day, but I have never wanted to be anything else.

At the age of seven, I got the opportunity to go to one of NASA's official Space Camps in Alabama. There, I learned everything I had been wanting to know about space, rockets, and Mars. The second time I went was the time I was given my call sign. (This is the nickname used to communicate with specific astronauts via radio.)

I wanted one of the blue flight suits that I saw many people wearing but was too little to fit into any of the regular ones. I ended up getting a deep blue knock-off version. When I wore it, everyone said I looked like a blueberry and kept calling me that throughout the day. So, it was decided that my call sign would be Blueberry!

To become an astronaut, there are many different tracks to take. Some are from the military and enjoy flying. Others come from a non-military life and are more focused on scientific research. Wherever you come from, you simply need a good education and practice in the field that you've chosen to get your degree in. (I hope to get my PhD in astrobiology.) Then you have to apply for NASA's selection programme and pass various physical and medical tests. The process is very difficult; so many people apply but only a handful are chosen. All of the training that I currently do isn't part of an official NASA astronaut programme. Instead, I do the things that I think will best benefit me in the future.

I chose to sit on a panel in Washington DC discussing future missions to Mars when I was 12 and I decided to be an ambassador for the Mars One programme that is aiming to set up a human colony on Mars. But my greatest achievement so far is the amount of kids I have gotten to speak to and the places I have been to spread the word about space.

It's so important that we get more girls interested in science, technology, engineering, and maths careers. In recent years, more women have been participating in the space industry, but that number should always be rising. At least now when astronauts are selected, the group has to be half men and half women.

If you have a **DREAM**,
NEVER GIVE UP on it and never
let anyone take it away from you.

Talk about what you want to do to the people around you. Family, friends, and even teachers can help a lot in getting you where you want to go. In the future, I want the world to come together and have bold goals that will allow us to explore further as a planet, instead of all the division that is happening today. In the next 20 years, I do believe that humans will have landed on the Red Planet, and I do believe that I will be one of them.

CIARA JUDGE, 21

SCIENTIST

Ciara Judge has always been naturally curious, but it wasn't until she was a teenager growing up in Ireland that science truly captured her heart. When her friend, Emer Hickey, noticed something odd about the peas growing in her garden, she and another friend, Sophie Healy-Thow, joined forces to make an astounding discovery that could help end world hunger!

Scientists told the trio it wouldn't work but years of experimenting in a bedroom proved the experts wrong and, in 2014, they won the grand prize at the Google Science Fair for showing how a particular bacteria could dramatically increase crop production. Together with Emer, Ciara founded her own company. Germinaid Innovations continues to research the effect of this wonder bacteria in the hope that suffering communities will eventually be able to grow and prosper from their own food.

Ciara is also an avid public speaker, lecturing on female and youth empowerment for organisations such as UNICEF and TEDx. Now studying genetics at university, it's no wonder *Time* magazine named her one of the world's most influential teens.

CIARA

In 2012, my friend Emer was gardening with her mum. When they pulled up their pea plants, they noticed weird growths on the roots. At the time, we were studying plant biology so we questioned our science teacher about what we had found. We were told that the growth were called nodules and were home to a bacteria called rhizobium. This bacteria forms a relationship with legume plants such as peas and beans, and turns atmospheric nitrogen into ammonia for the plant to use. In exchange, it gets a place to live.

Coincidentally, we were also learning about the ongoing food crisis and how humans would need to provide 50 per cent more food to feed the world by 2050. The developing world is suffering from food shortages and people are forced to live on high-starch diets of cereal crops. They struggle to grow enough to feed themselves and make a living. We wondered if we could use this superhero bacteria that we had just discovered to grow more useful crops.

All the signs told us that our theory wouldn't work. No evidence existed in scientific literature to back up the possibility, and experts told us not to waste our time. But after spending three years experimenting first in a lab we'd made in a spare bedroom and then in my back garden, we were able to increase crop productivity by more than 70 per cent.

It hit us that we had DISCOVERED SOMETHING that might actually CHANGE THE WORLD!

In the beginning, people underestimated us because of our age. But after we won the BT Young Scientist competition and the Google Science Fair, people started taking us more seriously. Emer and I wanted to continue our work so we started an agricultural research company. In 2016, we set up a lab at Bill Gates' Intellectual Ventures HQ in Seattle and hired an intern to carry out experiments for a year. We're learning more and more every day, and have even heard that other scientists are using our research to carry out further experiments.

One thing alone won't solve world hunger. Our discovery might just be a puzzle piece in a much more complex solution, but I'm happy for our research to have even contributed in the smallest way.

I've had a very unconventional journey and I'm proud to have come out the other side as a somewhat ordinary person. It would have been all too easy for my ego to blow up after getting a few hundred retweets. Don't get me wrong, I have felt the pressure to be a whiz kid. But I've also made sure that I'm always in a healthy headspace.

I want to inspire other young people to unlock their power. That's why I regularly speak at events around the world and visit schools. STEM is so instrumental in shaping every aspect of our lives, so it's vital that women have a voice in the decisions being made too. Unfortunately, there still aren't enough women in these sectors, but I'd like to counter that sad fact with a message of hope. The change is slow but it's happening. Years ago, my mum would have had to go to a boys' school to take a technical subject. Now, those subject choices are available for everyone.

Be brave and remember that bravery is not something you're born with. It can be practised every day.

So if you have a QUESTION that you're TOO AFRAID to ask in class, STICK YOUR HAND up and make yourself ASK IT.

And don't let your role models be mysterious characters. Find their email and get in contact with them. You'll be surprised how often you get a reply.

Whatever you do, don't feel the pressure to be the fountain of all knowledge. You'll never get to a point where you know absolutely everything. To quote the great artist Michelangelo: "I am still learning." If he was always learning, you can bet we will be too.

DON'T LET YOUR
ROLE MODELS BE
MYSTERIOUS
CHARACTERS.
FIND THEIR EMAIL
AND GET IN CONTACT
WITH THEM.

YOU'd BE SURPRISED
HOW OFTEN YOU'LL
GET A REPLY.

CIARA JUDGE

JULIE SEVEN SAGE, 14

ASTROPHYSICIST-IN-TRAINING, SCIENCE COMMUNICATOR

Some young people who are fascinated by space aspire to be an astronaut. But Julie Seven Sage is different. She wants to study the up above, from down below. At the age of five, she was pointing out errors in science books. And when she turned ten, she took her first Harvard University course, passing it with flying colours. Now 14, she has her own YouTube channel, 7 Sage Labs, filled with the coolest science news.

All of this caught the attention of NASA. Julie became part of the Cubes in Space programme; an initiative asking people to propose miniature experiments that can fit inside a small plastic cube. Three of Julie's ideas were selected and launched into space either on a rocket or in a high-altitude balloon. Her results could be used to improve spacecraft and day-to-day life for space explorers.

It's impossible to list all of Julie's achievements but it is possible to demonstrate her drive to help others. Whether it's teaching the public at her local observatory, inventing a filtration device that could provide clean drinking water for struggling areas, or showing young girls that a teenage scientist can feature in a Marvel comic, she's a lively and necessary face in the ever-growing world of STEM.

JULIE

One day, I walked up to my dad and proclaimed I knew what I wanted to do when I grew up. He asked if I wanted to be an astronaut. I said no, because it's too dangerous. He asked if I wanted to be an astronomer and, again, I said no. I told him that I wanted to know how all the stars moved, how things like black holes worked, and all of the calculations behind the universe. I decided I wanted to be an astrophysicist at six years old.

When I was in first grade, I constantly interrupted my teacher to either correct her or shout out random facts. We made a deal that if I stopped, I could say a science fact to the entire class at the end of every day. I have been sharing those awesome facts ever since. Now, I do it on YouTube too. It's a challenge because adults don't usually like getting news from children or assume my videos won't be of a high quality. But it takes a long time to produce them.

First, I have to find an interesting article or study to talk about and then I read everything about it to get a better understanding. The next step is to write a script, film the video, and put it through post-production where the green screen and effects are added. I have around a hundred scripts that I was never able to film, because their topics became too old. However, I definitely plan to continue my channel, and who knows what it'll grow to be!

My parents are very science-oriented, so I learn a lot from them as well as the internet. The online world is almost a gateway to the entirety of human knowledge. Many of us today take it

for granted because we grew up with it. It's easy to forget how important it is and how lost we'd be without it.

Our generation can also have little interest in STEM. Many people are taught that these subjects are only for "smart" people, so they automatically cross them off their list of interests. Then there's all of the ridicule and exclusion that people get when they're in the STEM world.

Being bullied is really hard to deal with, especially when it happens for multiple years. Luckily, I'm part of an amazing STEM community on Twitter and Instagram. A few of us teenage girls have a group called The STEAM Squad (the "A" has recently been added to represent the arts). Our goal is to help and support one another, and inspire and encourage kids to go in to STEAM by showing a group of kids doing things, rather than a group of unrelatable adults.

If you're the **FIRST** to do something, **BE PROUD**, even when things go wrong.

You are a leader and failure can be hard for anyone to accept; I have issues with it. But failure is necessary for learning. Without it, you can't improve yourself. And improving yourself is one of the best things you can do.

MAANASA MENDU, 16

INVENTOR

A standard daily routine goes something like this: you wake up, look at your phone, have a shower, eat breakfast and make your way to school, college, university, or work. Come night time, you switch on the lights, eat dinner, and watch TV. But have you ever thought about what it might be like to not have the resources to do any of that?

Maanasa Mendu has experienced it. Every year, she visits family in India and is always surprised at how little electricity her relatives have access to. And it's not just India that's struggling. Over a billion people in the world don't have access to the things we take for granted day in, day out.

When Maanasa was just 13, she found a solution: a $5 (£3.80) device that had the ability to transform sun, wind, and rain into actual power. Naming it HARVEST, she got to work. And in 2016, her scientific efforts won her the title of America's Top Young Scientist.

With support and funding, Maanasa is now hoping to introduce this renewable energy device to countries across the globe. It's so easy to use that anyone can be taught how to create their own power, and it is so cheap that money needn't be an issue.

Of course, Maanasa isn't done there. After securing HARVEST's future, she hopes to use her skills to invent other problem-solving devices. Devices that will hopefully, in years to come, mean that no country will ever need to be called "developing" ever again.

MAANASA

I first became interested in science during middle school. At the time, I had great teachers who showed me that science really does go beyond the classroom and I realised that science could be fun when I took part in Science Olympiad.

My first real project, however, was a serious one. Every summer, my family travels to India to visit my grandmother's village. She lives in a pretty remote area that has frequent blackouts, stopping access to lighting and air conditioning. I soon realised that this darkness was a permanent reality for around one billion people in the world.

People should be aware of the problems that those in other nations are suffering with. Around one in seven people lack access to electricity, directly influencing the level of education, healthcare, and even clean water that they receive. To solve this problem, we must be vocal advocates and not only invest in inexpensive and practical technology but also ensure it's being applied.

I came up with one such solution in 2013. At the time, I was reading about the JR East railway station in Japan and its piezoelectric floors. The piezoelectric effect is the ability of certain materials to generate an electric charge when subjected to mechanical stress such as compression. I had no idea then that this effect could be a solution to the energy crisis, but thought that gathering kinetic energy that would otherwise be wasted was an interesting idea.

First, I experimented with harvesting electricity from tiles that use this piezoelectric effect. Afterwards, I had the idea of using the effect to gather wind in a new way. Then I thought about integrating solar in to the mix to create something that could work in any weather condition and be applied across the globe. I called it HARVEST.

I am inspired by a number of scientists. Marie Curie, the award-winning physicist responsible for researching radiation treatment for cancer, was not only a revolutionary in her field, but also overcame male discrimination and continues to inspire female scientists around the world. It was while reading a biography on her that I came across the piezoelectric effect; it's interesting how history can transform science. Rachel Carson also inspires me. She was a vocal scientist who researched the environmental effects of the insecticide DDT, going against society's beliefs in order to transform the world.

Eventually, I hope to be able to use my device's renewable energy to provide an emergency power source for developing countries. I'm also looking to use the piezoelectric effect in different ways and have a bunch of other problem-solving ideas too. My long-term plan is to pursue STEM fields either as an environmental engineer or a physician scientist. Either way, I want to make a difference in our world.

If you have an idea,
JUST TRY IT.

Don't hesitate to sketch out a model or build a prototype using materials you can easily find at home. Your theory may seem crazy but you will never know if it could change a person's life if you don't try. You'll be surprised at what you can accomplish when you put your fears aside, so be brave and remember to take risks. Everyone has the potential to change the world for the better. The hard part is just harnessing it!

GITANJALI RAO, 13
SCIENTIST

In 2014, a scandal arose in the waters of Flint in Michigan, US. After the city changed its water source to a cheaper one, the water supply quickly became contaminated with lead. Residents were forced to use bottled or filtered water for everyday tasks including cooking, showering, and drinking. Gitanjali Rao was eight when she first began following the crisis. She found out that lead poisoning was a real thing and that millions of children around the world were suffering from it.

One day, she noticed her own parents testing her house's water supply for lead. She figured there had to be a cheaper, quicker, and more accurate way to detect the presence of this dangerous metal. So, she went about inventing one. With the help of a scientist mentor, she came up with Tethys: a portable device that can analyse water in seconds and send the results straight to your phone.

In 2017, this won her a $25,000 (approximately £20,000) prize and earned her the title of America's Top Young Scientist in the Discovery Education 3M Young Scientist Challenge. She was also awarded another $25,000 (£19,000) after winning the 2018 Paradigm World Challenge. Instead of blowing all that cash, Gitanjali worked on making her invention accessible to all and came up with more ways to improve the health of every living thing on the planet.

With plans to cure diseases and stop devastating outbreaks, she is the definition of a scientific revolutionary.

GITANJALI

Pollution – whether it's air, water, earth, or noise – is a growing man-made problem with major health impacts. Take the Flint water crisis. When I first heard about it on the news, I decided to follow it. Then I saw my own parents testing for lead in our water.

I saw that using test strips would take quite a few tries in order to produce accurate results. It also took days for results to be returned, meaning people had to wait to see if their water was contaminated. I wanted to do something to change this, not only for my parents but for the residents of Flint and places like Flint around the world.

I knew my idea was very complex, so was reluctant to start it at first. But I decided to give it a try. I sat down for a month and researched, planning out my entire device. It's based on something called carbon nanotube sensor technology and provides instant results on your mobile phone. The cartridge in the device is doped with chloride ions. When this is dipped into water with lead, the lead binds to these ions, forming lead chloride molecules. These then increase the resistance to the flow of current. With more research, I found that the more resistance to the current, the more lead there was in the water.

I named the finished creation Tethys after the Greek goddess of fresh water and am now working to improve its accuracy. I've also worked on several other ideas, including an anti-bullying app, artificial intelligence that could save gorillas, and a solution for adolescent depression.

I have even created a second potentially life-changing device. I heard a news report about rural villagers living in Africa and Asia who were ignoring snake bites because it was very difficult for them to access a doctor. Ignoring a snake bite often results in death, so I tried to find a way that would help people know if they needed medical assistance. Snakes inject different toxins into a person's body and each of these have different heat signatures. My device, Asclepius, uses non-contact thermography technology to scan an image of the bite and determine if it is venomous as well as the type of venom that has been injected, allowing people to act quickly and lives to be saved.

It doesn't matter what others think of us;

 what **MATTERS** is what **YOU LIKE** to do.

Our generation is growing up in a world where problems like space debris, climate change, overpopulation, and pollution exist. Innovation therefore needs to be part of our daily life and education. It is as important as maths and reading.

In the beginning of my scientific journey, I was afraid to ask or try. I didn't want to accept help because I was afraid of receiving a "no". I didn't want to try because I was afraid I would fail. Now that I've experienced both, I've realised that failure is just another step to success. "No" is the worst thing you can hear but remember that sooner or later, it will be a "yes".

ALLIE WEBER, 13

INVENTOR

When Allie Weber was eight years old, a toy company created a doll in her image. That's how important her work had already become. From the age of four, she was inventing, later becoming one of the loudest young voices the STEM world has to offer.

Allie's inventions don't aim to be part of a future solution to world issues such as starvation or cancer but they can be used to solve smaller, but no less significant, problems right now. The young inventor has come up with a temperature-sensing glove that can prevent frostbite and a medical device that makes lung therapy less daunting for young hospital patients. And when her school told her she was unable to wear a backpack, she transformed a rule-abiding bag into one that wouldn't damage children's spines due to the weight of their schoolbags.

Social media has become Allie's weapon of choice. She shouts the praises of fellow teen inventors and asks adults in the industry tough questions. She also has a YouTube channel, Tech-Nic-Allie Speaking, which shows off her inventions to inspire other keen young minds.

With hopes of becoming everything from an entrepreneur, engineer, and palaeontologist to a rocket scientist and movie director, the world had better watch out for Allie

Weber. Because with her around, there won't be many problems left to solve.

ALLIE

I'm privileged to have an analytical dad and creative mum, so I guess I'm the product of tossing them both together. Making things and breaking things in order to solve problems has always seemed so fun to me and, at the age of four, I was working with cardboard and even a hot glue gun to make castles, rockets, cars and boats.

A year later, I wanted to make a robot for my school science fair, but my parents thought it would be too difficult. So the next winter, I went to the basement and created a robot that was almost as tall as I was. My parents never underestimated me again.

What I most like to do is inspire others by making. There's a stereotype that an innovation is only a good one when it's a world-changing solution to a big problem. I didn't see anyone that looked like me doing what I was doing so started a YouTube channel, which allowed me to show that all kinds of creations can be successful.

It's odd that tech is seen as a boy's thing when the first computer programmers were female. That idea came with the dawn of the personal computer and an early advert for computers showed a boy confidently using one while a girl simply looked confused.

We are still FIGHTING those STEREOTYPES today.

I used to think that the 'pinkifying' of STEM toys for girls was one of them. But I now understand why that happens. We need all types of people with us if we want to engineer a world that's for everyone. I'm a girl who doesn't like pink but there are many girls who do. If I was the only girl who ended up in engineering, how would I design well for a woman who loves pink?

There were a couple of years where I felt like I didn't fit in, but I'm so blessed to now have an online community support system. I and some of my friends launched a website called The STEAM Squad. Our mentors told us not to show up to the table alone, so we show other girls how to build a network and be advocates for STEAM.

Juggling my inventing work with YouTube, school, and everything else takes a toll on how much energy I have. So it's a good thing there's chocolate milk to wake me up in the morning! But the older I get, the more schoolwork there is, so I think this will be the one thing that holds me back in the future.

But I've come to realise that something doesn't have to change the world to change your life. It wasn't one of my top award-winning inventions that got me cast in the TV series, *Mythbusters Jr*. It was a strap I had made for my school bag out of an old backpack. So, you can solve the problems you see around you with what you have. You'd be amazed at how many innovations started with nothing more than cardboard!

SOMEthing
doesn't HAVE
TO Change THE
World TO
Change Your
LifE.

ALLiE WEBER

RESOURCES

ABBIE BARNES
Song Thrush Productions:
https://www.songthrushproductions.co.uk/
Twitter: @AbbieSongThrush
Facebook: Abbie Barnes / Song Thrush
Productions
YouTube: Abbie Barnes | Song Thrush Productions

ALLIE WEBER
Twitter: @RobotMakerGirl
Instagram: @tech_nic_allie
YouTube: Tech-nic-Allie Speaking
The STEAM Squad:
http://www.thesteamsquad.org/

ALYSSA CARSON
Website: https://nasablueberry.com/
Twitter: @NASABlueberry1
Instagram: @nasablueberry
Facebook: @nasablueberry
Project PoSSUM: https://projectpossum.org/
Mars One: https://www.mars-one.com/

AMANDA SOUTHWORTH
Astra Labs: https://withastra.com/
Twitter: @amndasuthwrth / @withastra
Instagram: @withastra
Kode With Klossy:
https://www.kodewithklossy.com/

AMELIA ROSKIN-FRAZEE
Website: http://www.aroskinfrazee.com/
The Make It Safe Project:
https://www.makeitsafeproject.org/
Twitter: @ARoskinFrazee / @MakeItSafeLGBT
GLSEN: https://www.glsen.org/
No Red Tape Columbia: http://noredtapecu.org/

AMIKA GEORGE
Free Periods: https://www.freeperiods.org/
Twitter: @AmikaGeorge
Instagram: @freeperiods
The Pink Protest: https://www.pinkprotest.org/
Bloody Good Period:
https://www.bloodygoodperiod.com/

Plan International: https://plan-uk.org/
Freedom4Girls: https://www.freedom4girls.co.uk/

ARIA WATSON
Twitter: @AriarWatson
Instagram: @a.riawatson /
@ariawatsonphotography
YouTube: AriArWatson

ASHA & IMA CHRISTIAN
Five-O: http://fiveo.us/
Dreamer Babe: https://www.dreamerbabe.com/
Twitter: @AshaTalia / @thenames_ima
Instagram: @ashatalia / @thenames_ima
Mapping Police Violence:
https://mappingpoliceviolence.org/
Girls Who Code: https://girlswhocode.com/

BANA ALABED
Twitter: @AlabedBana
Instagram: @alabed_bana
Website: https://bana-alabed.com

CIARA JUDGE
Website: http://ciarajudge.com/
Twitter: @CiaraFudgyJudgy
Instagram: @ciarajudge
Google Science Fair:
https://www.googlesciencefair.com/
BT Young Scientist: https://btyoungscientist.com/
Intellectual Ventures:
http://www.intellectualventures.com/
We Are Family Foundation:
http://www.wearefamilyfoundation.org/

COREY MAISON
Instagram: @coreymaison
Facebook: Corey Maison
YouTube: Corey Maison
Stand with Trans: http://standwithtrans.org/

DEJA FOXX
Twitter: @Deja_Foxx
Instagram: @dejafoxx
Website: https://dejafoxx.weebly.com/

Planned Parenthood:
https://www.plannedparenthood.org/
International Planned Parenthood Federation:
https://www.ippf.org/

DIANA SIROKAI
Instagram: @dianasirokai

ELLA FIELDS
YouTube: Ella Fields
Twitter: @elllafields
Instagram: @elllafields
Vimeo: https://vimeo.com/308392533

ELLEN JONES
Website: https://www.ellen-jones.co.uk/
Twitter: @ellen__jones
Instagram: ellen__jones
YouTube: @needforcaffeine

GITANJALI RAO
Twitter: @gitanjaliarao
Young Scientist Lab:
https://www.youngscientistlab.com/
The Paradigm Challenge:
https://www.projectparadigm.org/

HANNAH CAMILLERI
Girls Against: http://girlsagainst.org.uk/
Twitter: @hann_jvc / @girlsagainst
Instagram: @hann.jvc / @girls.against
Facebook: @girlsagainstgroping

HANNAH HERBST
Website: http://www.hannahherbst.com/
Twitter: @hannahherbst07
World Science Fair:
https://www.worldsciencefestival.com/

HEBH JAMAL
Twitter: @hebh_jamal
Instagram: @hebh_jamal
Muslim American Society:
https://www.muslimamericansociety.org/
Integrate NYC:
https://www.integratenyc.org/

HOLLY JACOBSON
Fancy Pants Films:
http://www.fancypantsfilms.co.uk/
Twitter: @holly_butterfly
Facebook: @fancypantsfilmsUK

ISABEL & MELATI WIJSEN
Bye Bye Plastic Bags:
http://www.byebyeplasticbags.org/
Twitter: @BBPB_bali
Instagram: @melatiwijsen / @isabel.wijsen /
@byebyeplasticbags
Facebook: @byebyeplasticbags

JAMIE MARGOLIN
Zero Hour: http://thisiszerohour.org
Twitter: @Jamie_Margolin / @ThisIsZeroHour
Instagram: @jamie_s_margolin / @thisiszerohour
Facebook: @ThisIsZeroHour
Our Children's Trust:
https://www.ourchildrenstrust.org/

JASILYN CHARGER
One Mind Youth Movement:
https://www.omym.org/
International Indigenous Youth Council:
https://indigenousyouth.org/
Twitter: @iiycfamily
Instagram: @iiycfamily
Facebook: @IIYCFamily

JORDAN REEVES
Born Just Right: https://www.bornjustright.org/
Twitter: @jordanjustright / @bornjustright
Instagram: @jordanjustright / @bjrorg
Facebook: @jordanjustright / @bornjustright
Camp No Limits: https://nolimitsfoundation.org/

JULIE SEVEN SAGE
Website:
http://www.supernovastylesciencenews.com/
Twitter: @Supernova_Style / @7SageLabs
Instagram: @supernovastylesciencenews /
@7sagelabs
Facebook: @SupernovaStyleScienceNews
YouTube: 7 Sage Labs
Cubes in Space:
http://www.cubesinspace.com/

KADEEJA KHAN
Twitter: @Emeraldxbeautyy
Instagram: @emeraldxbeauty
YouTube: EmeraldxBeauty

KARI LAWLER
Twitter: @KariLawler / @Youth4AI
Instagram: @karilawler
UK Space Agency Twitter: @spacegovuk

KATIE SONES
Lipslut: https://www.lipslut.com/
Twitter: @Hello_Lipslut
Instagram: @katie.sones / @hello.lipslut
Facebook: @Lipslut
Human Rights Campaign: https://www.hrc.org/
National Organisation for Women: https://now.org/
American Civil Liberties Union: https://www.aclu.org/

KEHKASHAN BASU
Green Hope Foundation:
http://greenhopefoundation.wixsite.com/greenhope
Twitter: @KehkashanBasu / @GreenHopeYouth
Instagram: @kehkashan5basu
Facebook: @greenhopeyouth.greenhopefoundation
United Nations Environment:
https://www.unenvironment.org/
International Children's Peace Prize:
https://childrenspeaceprize.org

LANE MURDOCK
National School Walkout:
https://www.nationalschoolwalkout.net/
Walkout To Vote: https://walkouttovote.org/
Twitter: @lanemurdock2002 / @schoolwalkoutUS / @FutureCoalition
Instagram: @lanemurdock / @nationalwalkout
Facebook: @thefuturecoalition
March For Our Lives:
https://marchforourlives.com/

LILLY PLATT
Twitter: @lillyspickup
Instagram: @lillys_plastic_pickup
Facebook: @lillysplasticpickup
HOW Global: http://www.howglobal.org/
Plastic Pollution Coalition:
https://www.plasticpollutioncoalition.org/
World Cleanup Day:

https://www.worldcleanupday.org/
Your Straw: https://yourstrawbamboostraws.com/

LILY MADIGAN
Twitter: @lesbianleftie
Instagram: @lilytessamadigan

MAANASA MENDU
Twitter: @MaanasaMendu02

MADELINE STUART
Website: http://www.madelinestuartmodel.com/
21 Reasons Why: https://www.21reasonswhy.shop/
Twitter: @Madeline_Stuart
Instagram: @madelinesmodelling_
Facebook: @madelinesmodelling
Global Down Syndrome Foundation:
https://www.globaldownsyndrome.org/

MADDY RASMUSSEN
Safe Place Project:
https://www.safeplaceproject.com/
Legal Voice: http://www.legalvoice.org/
National Network of Abortion Funds:
https://abortionfunds.org/
Center for Reproductive Rights:
https://www.reproductiverights.org/
Marie Stopes International:
https://www.mariestopes.org/

MARIA OSADO
Güerxs: http://guerxs.odie.us/
Instagram: @guerxs

MARY GRACE HENRY
Reverse The Course:
http://www.reversethecourse.org/
World of Children: https://worldofchildren.org/

MAYA GHAZAL
Twitter: @GhazalMia
Instagram: @ghazalmia
The Children's Society:
https://www.childrenssociety.org.uk/
The Diana Award: https://diana-award.org.uk/
UNHCR, the UN Refugee Agency:
http://www.unhcr.org/

MC SOFFIA
Instagram: @mcsoffia
Facebook: @mcsoffia
YouTube: MC Soffia

MEMORY BANDA
Website: https://memorybanda.blogspot.com/
Twitter: @Memorybanda75
Girls Empowerment Network Malawi:
http://www.genetmalawi.org
Girls Not Brides: https://www.girlsnotbrides.org/
Girl Up: https://www.girlup.org

MIKAILA ULMER
Me & the Bees Lemonade:
https://www.meandthebees.com/
Twitter: @MikailasBees
Instagram: @mikailasbees
Facebook: @MikailasBees

MILLICENT SIMMONDS
Instagram: @milliesimm
National Institute on Deafness and Other
Communicative Disorders:
https://www.nidcd.nih.gov/

MILLY EVANS
I Support Sex Education:
https://www.isupportsexeducation.com/
Twitter: @millyelizabethe / @ISupportSexEd
Instagram: @isupportsexeducation
Family Planning Association:
https://www.fpa.org.uk/
Stonewall: http://www.stonewall.org.uk/

MUZOON ALMELLEHAN
Twitter: @muzoonrakan1
Instagram: @muzoonalmellehan
UNICEF: https://www.unicef.org.uk/

NAWAAL AKRAM
Twitter: @NawaalAkram
Instagram: @nawaal.akram /
@muscular.dystrophy.middleeast
Mada: https://mada.org.qa

NOA GUR GOLAN
Women Wage Peace:
http://womenwagepeace.org.il/en/
War Resisters' International:
https://www.wri-irg.org/en

SAGE GRACE DOLAN-SANDRINO
Twitter: @graceadvocates
The Aspen Institute:
https://www.aspeninstitute.org/
White House Initiative on Educational
Excellence for African Americans:
https://sites.ed.gov/whieeaa/
GLAAD: https://www.glaad.org/
National Black Justice Coalition:
http://nbjc.org/

TAYLOR RICHARDSON
Twitter @astrostarbright
Instagram: @astronautstarbright
Facebook: @astroStarBright
Space Camp: https://www.spacecamp.com/

WADI BEN-HIRKI
Wadi Ben-Hirki Foundation:
http://wbhfoundation.org/
Twitter: @wadibenhirki / @WBHFoundation
Facebook: @wbhfoundation
Instagram: @wadibenhirki /
@wadibenhirkifoundation
Global Partnership for Education:
https://www.globalpartnership.org/

ZOE ROSENBERG
Happy Hen Animal Sanctuary:
https://www.happyhen.org/
Twitter: @Zoe_Rooster
Instagram: @zoe_rooster /
@happy_hen_animal_sanctuary
Facebook: @HappyHenAnimalSanctuary

ACKNOWLEDGEMENTS

To every young woman who contributed to this book, I am eternally grateful for the time you gave to me and the efforts you have gone to, and will continue to go to, to make the world a fairer and more positive place. I feel extremely privileged to have been able to share your stories and hope that these pages will shout your messages loud and clear to people around the world.

And now comes the part that sounds like an Oscar speech. To all of the people from Wren & Rook who helped mould this book into what it is, to the brilliant artist that is Manjit Thapp, and to my agent, Hattie, who believed in it from the very beginning, I deeply thank you.

Of course, I can't forget the women who have inspired me for years: my mum who is currently promoting sustainability and equality to every person she encounters, my nan who is one of the most caring people I'll ever meet, and my sister and best friend who have both always been there to support me. Neither can I forget my dad or my partner who demonstrate how to be male allies to the feminist cause each and every day.

Words are of paramount importance but so is action to bring those words to life. That is something that I, and I hope many others, will continue to remember for years to come.